Survey of 300 A+ Students

Written By:

Kenneth Green

Published By:

Crème de la Crème Press
2342 Shattuck Avenue, No. 101,
Berkeley, CA. 94704-1517, USA
http://www.freewebs.com/honors

Survey of 300 A+ Students
Copyright @ 2003 by Kenneth Green

All rights reserved. No part of this book shall be reproduced, stored in a retrieval system, or transmitted by any means, electronic, mechanical, photocopying, recording, or otherwise without written permission from the publisher.

The A+ project is a subjective qualitative inquiry into the thoughts of some people who have at some point in their academic careers earned an A+ grade. It is not a quantitative academic or professional study. The survey project's methods; materials; images; tools; results; conclusions; comments; thoughts of or by survey participants; and comments or thoughts of or by the author are not standardized nor are they recommended. This publication is not a guide for students or teachers. The words, thoughts, and intentions presented in the book are not representative of any institution, the survey participants, the author, the artist, any person nor any entity. Any information associated with or suggested in association with an institution, person, or other entity should be verified for correctness and completeness with and permission acquired of the entity or an administrative representative of the entity before information is accepted or tools used. The internet sources, computer software or computer hardware suggested or listed, their purposes, permissions, requirements, availability, addresses, and their contents have not been verified by the author; are not recommended by the author; and may be time-sensitive. A computer voice is used for the articulation of text in one of the audio versions of the book. Therefore, some words, names, punctuation, dictations, accents, expressions, emphasis, and areas of emphasis may not be correct. Additional differences between written and audio versions of the book are to increase clarity of expression and understanding. Although every precaution has been taken in the preparation of this book, the publisher and author assume no responsibility for errors or omissions. No liability is assumed for damages resulting from the use of the information contained herein.

Author: Kenneth Green
Front Cover Artist: Andrew Twietmeyer

Published by Crème de la Crème Press, 2342 Shattuck Avenue, No. 101, Berkeley, CA. 94704-1517, USA. http://www.freewebs.com/honors

ISBN: 097238880X

An order form is on the last page of this book.

TABLE OF CONTENTS

SECTION	TITLE	PAGE
1	Introduction	1
2	What is an A+?	1
3	Goal	4
4	Before the Term	5
5	Beginning of the Term	27
6	Before Class	31
7	During Class	45
8	After Class	59
9	Before Test	125
10	During Test	131
11	After Test	143
12	Time	145
13	Lack of Interest	153
14	Stress	161
15	Finance	173
16	After Course	177
17	For Educators	179
18	Conclusion	189
Appendix A	Survey Questions	205
Appendices B-G	Online Sources	206
Appendix H	Survey Participants	209
Index		217

OUTLINE OF BOOK

SECTION 1: Introduction 1

SECTION 2: What is an A+? 1

SECTION 3: Goal 4

SECTION 4: Before the Term 5
    First Things First 5
    Finance 5
    Housing 6
    Major 8
    Choosing Classes 9
    Work 12
    Projects 12
    Preparing for Classes 13
    Moving onto Campus 18
    Priority Lists 19
    Accomplishing Goals 20
    To Do Lists 22
    Binders 24
    You Can Do It 25

SECTION 5: Beginning the Term 27

SECTION 6: Before Class 31
    Read 31
    Written Assignments 31
    Environment 32
    Reading 34
    Highlighting 39
    Underlining 39
    Other Material Before Class 40
    Other Actions Before Class 42

SECTION 7: During Class 45
    Attend Class 45
    Before Lecture Begins 47
    Beginning Lecture 48
    Respect Teacher 49
    Taking Notes in Class 50
    Lecture-note Format 51
    Amount to Write in Class 52
    Color 53
    Other Distinctions 53
    Shorthand 54
    Speed 55
    Slides 56
    Study the Teacher 56
    Five Senses 57
    End of Lecture 58

SECTION 8: After Class 59

SECTION 8A: Rewriting Notes 59
    Correcting Notes 60
    Merging the Notes 60
    Re-organizing Notes 61
    Test Format 61
    Note Cards 61
    Box Charts 62
    Tables 62
    Flow Charts 62
    Mind Maps 62
    Images 62
    Diagrams 62
    Illustrations 62
    Crunching the Rest 62
    Mnemonics 63
    Acronyms 63
    Acrostics 63
    Word Association 64
    Number Association 64
    Familiar Groupings 64
    Bridges 65
    Objects 65
    Common Sequence 65
    Examples 66
    Songs 66
    Overlap 66
    Confidence 66

SECTION 8B: Office Hours 67
    General Points 67
    When to Attend 67
    Specificity 68
    Probing 69
    Quality 69
    The Cutting Edge 69
    Stay In the Right Direction 70
    That Extra Something 70
    Corrections 70
    Demonstrate 72
    Objective and Subjective 72
    Benefit of the Doubt 73

One on One 73

SECTION 8C: About Assignments 75
    Start Today 75
    Give Yourself Instructions 75
    Right Question 75
    Intent of Assignment 75
    Previous Publication 76
    Cite Sources 76
    Relate to Everyday Life 77
    Relate to Industry 77
    Search the Internet 78
    Through the Teacher's Eyes 82
    Creativity 82
    Across Lines 83
    Hard Part Verses Easy Part 83
    Storage 83
    Serious About Everything 84
    Learn It Now 85
    Understand It 85
    Question Yourself 86
    Trial and Error 86
    Pros and Cons 87
    Units of Measurement 87
    Chaos to Categories 88
    Context 88
    What You Will Do Next 89
    Step-by-Step Method 89
    Practice Makes Perfect 90
    Practice Questions 91
    Working in a Group 93
    Show Your Work 93
    Repetition 94
    Repetition with Shrinkage 94
    Four-times Approach 94
    Seven-times Approach 95
    Previous Two Lessons 95
    Previous Week 95
    Same Day 96
    Bed 96
    Morning 96
    Write It 96
    Type It 97
    Note Cards 97
    Post-It Notes 98
    Mneumonics 98
    Use the Same Numbers 99
    Images 99
    Say it Outloud 99
    Act it Out 100
    Play Games 100
    Give Him What He Wants? 100
    Presentations 101
    Monitor Progress 102

SECTION 8D: Writing Assignments 103

SECTION 8E: Dissertation 111

SECTION 8F: Arts 119
    Master the Fundamentals 119
    Rehearse Related Forms 119
    In Isolation & Together 120
    Mentally Rehearse 120
    Remain Loose 120
    Identify Details 121
    Continuous Refinement 121
    Instinct 121
    Exchange Information 121
    Learn the History and Culture 121
    Landmarks 122
    Personal Experience 122
    Create Your Style 122
    Reverse Your Perception 123
    Believe Yourself 123
    Outcomes 123

SECTION 9: Before Test 125
    What Will It Cover? 125
    Review 125
    The Night Before Test 128
    Sleep 128
    Morning of the Examination 129
    In the Test Room 130

SECTION 10: During Test 131
    General Advice 131
    Essay Questions 134
    Short-answer Questions 136
    Multiple-Choice 137
    Matching Format 139
    Remembering Things 139
    Extras 140
    Summarize 140
    Last but Not Least 141

SECTION 11: After Test 143
    Celebrate 143
    Check the Grading 143
    Assess the Assessment 143
    Learn From the Results 144

SECTION 12: Time 145
- Evaluate Use of Time 145
- Use Each Day 145
- Extra Time in the Day 146
- Combine Tasks 146
- Switch Subjects 147
- Make a Regular Schedule 147
- Last Minute 148
- A bit behind? 148
- Little Time Left? 148
- Place it in One Document 151
- Use Reference Librarian 152
- Sleep Less? 152
- Extensions 152
- Dishonesty? 152

SECTION 13: Lack of Interest 153
- Facilitating Activity 153
- Find the Interesting Parts 155
- What U Love 155
- Those Who Love It 156
- Take It With a Friend 157
- Interest Through a Tutor 157
- Help Others 158
- Pretend 158
- Read Out Loud 159
- Pure Learning 159
- It is Not Forever 160
- Get it Off Your Chest 160
- Make it a Top Priority 160

SECTION 14: Stress 161
- Deep Breathing 161
- Good State of Mind 161
- Take a Nap 162
- Find Private Time 162
- Positive Relationships 162
- Be Disrespected 163
- Morning on the Day Before 163
- Clean Your Environment 164
- Start From Where You Are 164
- Physical Activity 164
- Other Activities 165
- Diet 165
- Keep Busy 166
- Pretending 167
- Some Stress 167
- Translate the Stress 167
- Run Towards the Challenge 168
- Don't Compare to Others 167
- Condition Yourself 168
- Coach Yourself 168

SECTION 15: Finance 173
- General Advice 173
- Money From Others 174
- Jobs 174

SECTION 16: After Course 177
- General Advice 177
- Storage 177
- Keep Going 178
- Congratulation 178

SECTION 17: For Educators 179
- Learn from History 179
- What is Important to You? 179
- Be Organized 180
- Sound and Letter Size 181
- Enthusiasm 182
- Don't Read Lectures 182
- Clarity 183
- Complete Notes 183
- Order 184
- Objectiveness 184
- Assumptions, Tradition, Etc. 184
- Examples 185
- Challenges 185
- Amount of Work 186
- Clearly Define Goals 186
- Get The Student There 187
- Legitimate Problems 187
- Derogatory Words 187
- Respect is a Two-way Street 187
- Order of Scrutiny 188
- Written Corrections 188
- Availability 188

SECTION 18: Conclusion 189

Appendix A: Survey Questions 205
Appendix B: Searching Publications 206
Appendix C: Writing Tools 206
Appendix D: Primary Sources 207
Appendix E: Research Ideas 208
Appendix F: Images and Maps 208
Appendix G: Journalists' Tools 208
Appendix H: Survey Participants 209

Index 217
Order Form 221

SECTION 1: INTRODUCTION

The purpose of the A+ survey listed in Appendix A was to acquire information about some thoughts, beliefs, strategies, and actions of some students who have earned an A+ grade. This survey was given to 300 students at the college level or higher who have at some point in their academic careers earned an A+ grade or an equivalent mark. The list of participants is in Appendix H. The vast majority are American. Some are from other countries, including Australia, Botswana, Canada, China, Denmark, Egypt, England, France, Israel, Japan, Kenya, Poland, and Portugal.

The book is articulated from a college perspective but applies to other academic levels. It is, for the most part, a qualitative inquiry into the thoughts of some people who have earned an A+ grade but it is not a comprehensive study guide for students. Trends in the survey responses will be presented. Some of the ideas will be useful for some people but not for others.

SECTION 2: WHAT IS AN A+?

Some participants offered a variety of technical descriptions of A+. Some presented A+ in terms of percentage cut-off points on an absolute scale. Most of the percentage cut-off points presented by students at American colleges were 95% or above. In some cases, the A+ grade was reserved for students who earned a score of 100%. The described percentage differences between an A and an A+ in classes ranged from 0.01% to 10%. One participant pointed out that at many Chinese colleges, scores between 80% and 90% are equivalent to an A and scores above 90% are equivalent to an A+. A British student said that at many colleges in England, 70% is the cut-off point for an A and scores above 80% are equivalent to an A+; assessments are difficult by design. Other absolute scales were described. A student in Denmark explained that many colleges there use an absolute scale of 0 to 13, where 11 is an A, 12 is not applied, and 13 is an A+. A student in Portugal stated that it is common there for colleges to use a grading scale from 1 to 20, where 19 is an A and 20 is an A+.

Some relative scales were described too. One example is the use of standard deviations from the mean. A student at the University of California at Berkeley mentioned that he earned an A+ in a class where the A/B cut-off point was defined as one and one-half standard deviations above the mean of the class and the A/A+ cut-off point was defined as one and three-fourths standard deviations above the mean. He stated, "The cut-off points for standard deviation based scales are usually subjectively chosen by the teacher, the department, or course tradition. There is no objective cut-off point in part because of the laws of statistics; the decision of cut-off point has to be subjective." There were two other relative-scale scenarios presented by students. In one, the A+ grade is given to the top one to three students when they score significantly higher than the class; here, the level of statistical significance is subjectively chosen. The other scenario is one in which the student is given an A+ when he or she meets both a high absolute standard and a high relative standard.

These responses from students illustrate differences in the technical measures of an A+. Different forms of absolute and relative scales are used. There are also differences in points allocated for credit. For example, some students described receiving 4.0 grade points per unit of credit for an A or an A+ grade. Students at other schools received 4.0 grade points per unit of credit for an A but 4.33 grade points per unit of credit for an A+. Some students meet their teacher's measure of an A+ but the administrations of their schools do not provide a method of recognizing the mark on academic transcripts.

Many of the participants in the survey described A+ in non-technical terms, such as: thoroughly accomplishing the goals that the teacher sets and exceeding them; doing the expected work but also synthesizing novel ideas, interpretations, approaches, or pathways; looking for answers everywhere, not only in traditional places; adding insightful elements and finishing touches; doing extra credit work; offering to create their own extra credit work and depicting what they've learned from it; relating the material to other material; combining formulas and principles; proving ideas in more than one way; going beyond formal and conceptual boundaries; presenting the information at or beyond a professional level; identifying, exploring, and re-evaluating assumptions or limits; being able to teach it to or train others; furthering the teacher's knowledge of the topic in some way; and developing ideas that benefit not only the topic but also the field of study, individuals, groups, regions, and/or societies at large. Course material often needs to be recalled effectively at test time and presented in a clear, genuine, thoughtful, and/or dignified way. Some students explained that the grader must also be willing and able to recognize exceptional performance and to articulate or mark it so that other people can recognize it too. Some students asserted that the true A+ is the knowledge that they've done their best.

Qualitative descriptions of the difference between an A and an A+ included the following: one tier; small mistakes; a warm fuzzy feeling; icing on the cake; the belief that great is not good enough; the degree of consistency of high performance; the level of investment, dedication, exploration of the subject, precision, and refinement; ability, time, effort, motivation, and desire to learn or master the material; the extra push that says that you did the best that you could; and knowing that you nailed it before the transcripts come out. The difference between an A and an A+ was also represented as the difference between great and the best; near perfection and perfection; mere joy and ecstasy; delicious and superb; a fine meal, and a fine meal with fine wine and good company.

SECTION 3: GOAL

There were three basic trends in the data on the students' goals. For some students, the goal was to earn an A+ (or a similar mark). They designed specific strategies to accomplish this goal. For others, the goal was not to earn an A+ but rather to genuinely learn the material to the best of their ability for personal enrichment and satisfaction; the A+ grade was only a positive side effect. A third trend represented students who set neither the goal of A+ nor the goal of learning the best. Theirs was the more general goal to do the best at whatever task they attempt.

SECTION 4: BEFORE THE TERM

4.1 First Things First

There are things that some students do before the academic term begins. One of the first is to settle issues that can affect student life on a regular basis. Some said that this first step is the creation and maintenance of a relationship with God. Some of the students provided specific quotations from their individual religions to support this belief.

4.2 Finance

An area of early activity for many of the students is resolution of financial issues. The advice of many students is to take advantage of school-related, public, and private financial resources. Students should also consider the financial possibilities of individual school departments, societies, fraternities, sororities, foundations, government agencies, and industry. Other resources include scholarships, grants, gifts, stipends, fellowships, assistantships, employer support, and student loans. Sometimes students make the mistake of only considering convenient sources in their immediate arena. As a result, they only receive a small fraction of what is available to people in their categories. Some of the survey participants suggested web sites where large databases of financial resources can be searched for free. These include scholarships.com, collegescholarships.com, fastweb.com, eduprep.com, and collegenet.com. One student suggested a U.S. government site, ed.gov/studentaid/student.html.

Students are advised to apply for more money than they think they'll need, as not all financial needs can be predicted in advance. In addition, sources often provide less than expected in terms of total amount, method of allocation, and timing of allocation. Students are strongly advised to apply at the earliest point. One student said, "Financial officers have many sources and a bubbly attitude early in the process but as time goes by, and sometimes early in the process, their resources and excitement to help you can readily dwindle. They are human too." A common mistake is for a student to apply for assistance a few months before their classes begin. In many cases, the decisions have been made. Even yet, many applications that have already been submitted may still await review. One student asserted that at his school, final decisions are sometimes made well before the official stated deadline for applications. His advice is to set a false deadline that is earlier than the official deadline, no matter what the student is applying for. This increases the student's competitiveness and protects the student from differences between written rules and actual practice.

In-State Status: One student moved to her university's state a year in advance and attained in-state status. The in-state status meant that her tuition was lower. In the year before she started college, she worked full time in this new state. The combination of in-state status, full-time work before the school year, and student loan money allowed her to cover the costs of school.

4.3 Housing

Housing is another area of early competition for students. Many colleges have space available on campus for less than twenty percent of their student body. Many of the participants argued the merits of on-campus housing. It can mean that class is only a few minutes away, increases the chance of getting to class early, and increases the chance of finding a seat where the student can see and hear well. In addition, on-campus housing allows quick access to meetings with faculty and students. It allows participation in activities that can make a difference between an A and an A+.

One student explained that she learned about off-campus housing the hard way. During her freshman year, she got an apartment that was a twenty-minute drive from campus. Each morning, she had to leave her apartment early to get through traffic. Once she got near campus, she found competition for parking spaces and could only park several blocks away. She walked from the parking space to her classroom on the other side of campus and ended up with a seat that blocked her view and made hearing difficult. With parking limitations she could only stay on campus for a short period of time. As she headed home, she dealt with similar problems in the opposite direction. With these regular limitations, she missed out on some laboratory sessions, class projects, student group meetings, review sessions, office hours, parts of some of her classes, and all of some of her classes. Her grades suffered but she arranged to move onto campus the next year.

Another student advised students to sign up for at minimum a single room. He originally shared a room; he found that his roommate was ready to play the stereo at times when he was ready to study. His roommate wanted to stay up when he wanted to sleep. If a student has his own room, he has the option to close the door. This student also suggested choosing a room whose walls are thick enough to block sound. Having thin walls can be similar to not having walls at all.

One student, who was scheduled to begin his first year of college in the fall, traveled to the state of his college nine months before the term began. He looked at one-bedroom apartments across the street from the campus; paid the manager a deposit, and first and last month's rent to secure an apartment for the fall; and returned home until then. "To get what you want," he advised, "start when it feels uncomfortably early. This is the signal that you are starting at the right time."

4.4 Picking a Major

Some of the participants explained how they picked a major. One student at the University of California at Santa Cruz insisted that it was important to her to find a major that leads to a truly fulfilling career. She did not want to drift into a major. So she presented six ideas to a career advisor at her university. The advisor suggested some ideas and helped bring her list down to four options. Her advisor then directed her to a computer database called "Career Advice Network," in the school's career center. This database lists alumni who are willing to answer questions about their careers. The student used it to contact alumni in the four remaining fields and ask them detailed questions. This information helped her narrow her decision down to her college major. Many schools are now beginning the process of connecting the students with the alumni database for career advice.

A student at the University of Illinois at Chicago got a list of all the degree subjects available in her university and ranked each on a scale of 0 to 100. She took the three highest ranked items and spoke to students and faculty members about their subjects. The student then re-ranked these three options and chose her major. Another student, at North Carolina State University, used an Internet database called "Career Key" at ncsu.edu/careerkey. Students using this database take what is called a "Career Key Measure" by answering questions online. The online computer program suggests career options based on the answers. The program then directs students to detailed descriptions of these career options. Another web site that provides career descriptions is located at bls.gov/oco/.

4.5 Choosing Classes

True Interest: Many students explained the importance of choosing a course of study that is close to your heart. It's easier to do well in classes in which you have an interest. You will remember more without trying. Things that are painful experiences for others will be enjoyable challenges to you. As the material in the course of study overlaps, things that you learn in one class will give you an advantage in the next class. A student at Stevens Institute of Technology picks classes in which he is interested and has some background. He said that this gives him two advantages and allows him to expand his expertise in these aggregate areas.

Level and Number of Classes: A participant who attended the University of California at Berkeley held that students should not hesitate to take a lower level class if that is where their experience is. She also argued that there is no need to rush through college in three or four years. She suggested that people will be more likely to judge the student in the future based on the grade in the class or the grade point average than on the level of the course. She decided in advance that she would graduate from college in five years (equivalent to ten academic terms at her university). She got a list of all of the classes that she was required to take to complete her major and to graduate. She divided this by ten terms and found that she needed to take three courses per academic term to achieve her goal. She focused on those few at a time. Five years later she graduated with a 4.1/4.0 grade point average. She said that no one ever asks about the level of difficulty of her courses, nor does anyone ask how long she was in college. However, they are impressed with her final grade point average; she was accepted to all of the graduate schools that she applied to. An anonymous student declared that sometimes admissions officers do not know the level of a course that a student has taken because each school has its own individual coding system for level of difficulty of course on academic transcripts; the admissions officers do not have the time nor the interest in looking up the code for every course on every application.

There were other comments from survey participants concerning the number of classes. Some students sign up for one more class per term than they plan to complete, and drop the one class that they like the least or are doing the worst in by the drop deadline of the term. Some take their hardest class of the year during the summer, allowing them to do a great job without the distraction of the other classes. This also reduces the academic load for the regular term. Other students sit in on a hard class one term before taking it for credit. The first time allows them to learn the ropes of the class. During the second exposure, the students know where to focus their energies and they get high grades.

Shorthand Class: A student at the University of Colorado said that one summer he took a course on shorthand. He took this course seriously and learned it thoroughly. With this new skill, he was able to keep up with fast moving lectures. It is a skill that will provide him with an advantage for the rest of his life.

Alternative Classes: "If you are stuck with a class that does not fit your interest," a student at Emory University said, "ask a dean if the class is really necessary for your course of study, and suggest an alternative class (like an independent study class). Remember, people who ask for more, get more, and the worst they can do is say 'no.'" One benefit of an independent study class is that sometimes the student can set up and receive credit for learning projects that are at least within striking range of an interest. These courses sometimes have greater flexibility in the scheduling of assignments; in some cases, such courses allow the student to decide when assignments are turned in and/or when examinations are taken. This can be one way to compensate for a lack of schedule flexibility in the student's other classes. At many schools, the student can do an internship and get academic credit for it; some students do this during the summer.

Evaluating the Course in Advance: Some students like to read the class description and then ask the professor in charge some targeted questions about the mechanics of the course before signing up for it. These questions include the following: What is the structure of the class? What are the main components of the class and how much weight is given to each component? How much of the course is taught by the professor? Who teaches the other parts of the course? What are the criteria for the distribution of grades? Who does the grading? How many examinations are there and what are their formats (multiple-choice, true-false, fill-in the blank, short-answer, essay, matching, open-book or closed-book)? What are the main assignments of the class and their formats? Is it possible to earn an A+ in this class? How often are A+'s and/or A's given? How many were given last term? What is expected of students? What are the time commitments?

It is ideal to be friendly and let the professor know that you appreciate her time in answering these questions. Some say that a professor can make or break a course; so as they communicate with the professor they attempt to absorb some information about the professor herself before picking the class. This includes information about the professor's personality, limitations, credentials, attitude towards teaching, attitude towards fairness, passion for the subject, teaching style, and clarity of presentation. Some students get some of this information by going to the department's web site and reading about the professor's background there. Some go further and search citation, periodical, bibliographical, or book review indexes which cover the field of study to find abstracts or other publications by or about the professor. Some students acquire information from other students who have taken the course by reading student-written evaluations, which are stored in the department or the department library, or by directly asking students who have taken the course some additional questions. These include the following: How many students dropped out of the course? What were the past assessments and grades like? Were they fair representations of what was taught in the class? Were you happy with your experience? Is there anything that I should be concerned about?

Targeted questions about the teaching and mechanics of the class can allow the student to determine, sometimes quickly, if the class is conducive to her learning and/or examination style. Sometimes knowing what to avoid is as important as knowing what to take. One student at Carnegie Mellon University explained that she determined which teaching method worked best for her and then committed herself to only signing up for classes with that particular teaching method. A student at Augsburg College mentioned that he feels like he is majoring in certain professors rather than subjects because he tends to only sign up for classes taught by the particular professors that he likes. He said that if you like the subject, like the professor, and know what he wants from you from previous experience, high grades come easy.

4.6 Work and Projects

Many students use the summer to work, do research, or pursue other projects; then they focus all the more on their classes during the regular term. Some students pick summer projects that complement their major or future career goals. For example, one student did computer research with a professor over a summer, funded by the Carnegie Foundation. His good work helped him understand the standards for research in his area of computer science, gain respect from faculty in his department, get published as a co-author in an excellent journal, and build credentials for his career.

Another way to begin building credentials before the term is to acquire a list of all awards available through the school, its affiliated organizations, and relevant outside organizations (like academic fraternities or sororities). Decide in advance which awards you would like to have by graduation. Review their criteria and requirements. Set the requirements as targets to be achieved by specific times in the path toward graduation. The same strategy can be used for post-graduate school, post-graduate training, and jobs. Acquire the application now, years before it is due. Look at the details on the application to see what specific things need to be accomplished by the time such applications must be turned in. Use the items on the application as targets to be accomplished by specific points in time in school. The application is a special tool because it provides both direct information about the things that are required and information about extra items that decision-makers like to see in the applicant's credentials. Many students do not find out about these extra items until they actually see the application itself in their final year; at that point, it is too late to build credentials in these areas.

4.7 Preparing for Classes Before the Academic Term Begins

"Once I get confirmation of my classes from the administration," a student at the University of California at Los Angeles explained, "I meet with the main professor of each class before the quarter for three reasons: to gather information; to gather materials; and to establish a rapport."

Gathering Information: "I tell the professor directly that I am interested in earning an A+ and I emphasize the word 'earn.' I ask for advice and tips on how to go about achieving this goal. I ask about any specific thresholds or standards, additional work I can do to grasp the true meaning of the subject, extra credit projects or other factors that I should consider while pursuing this goal. In some cases, this results in a specific and agreed upon format or target. Sometimes a format already exists. Then I define a plan for this or the professor helps me define one. Asking these questions also opens the professor's mind to the possibility of an A+ in association with my name. In some cases, a student who deserves an A+ gets an A by default because the professor is used to thinking in an A through F grade mode. Asking these questions can help to remind the professor that A+ is an option, if it is."

"I also probe the professor for areas of emphasis in the class and continue to do so through the course of the term for all assignments and examinations." Another student, from Clemson University, pointed out that "Different professors like different things. It's a simple fact of life. Two professors can teach the same class with the same objectives and focus on almost completely different topics." The student from the University of California at Los Angeles said, "I prioritize my study based on these areas of emphasis. In designing tests, some professors emphasize lecture material. Some emphasize the text(s). Others emphasize both. I ask the professor which will be emphasized on his tests. I have other questions for him: Are the students expected to memorize a large number of details or are they instead expected to explain principles and concepts? Is class participation part of the grading? There is not enough time in one quarter to thoroughly learn everything on a subject but there is enough time to learn areas that the professor deems important to learn at this stage of training on the subject. Many students make the mistake of emphasizing things that are deemed unimportant by the professor because they did not put forth an effort to find out what should be given more weight and what things should be given less weight. Other students make the mistake of trying to learn everything on the subject. As a result, they wear themselves out and end with a low grade. On every assignment, I pull one of the faculty or teaching assistants aside and probe for what is important here to direct my efforts and limited time. I ask myself the same questions: 'What is important to emphasize here? What are the take home messages? What is the smartest thing for me to do at this particular point in time, not five minutes ago?' If I think of a great idea, I ask myself if I can come up with an even greater idea in this moment. I also ask more than one person a question of interest because each person might only give part of the answer, and some parts of the answers may not be right. Asking several sources reveals the truth."

"I ask the professor to name the three best journals in his field; I read at least one article a week in one of these journals. I incorporate what I learn in these readings into my class assignments, homeworks, and test answers. This sets me apart from other students and lets the grader know that I am up-to-date."

Gathering Materials: "I also meet with the professor before the term to gather materials. These include study guide, syllabus, lecture notes, book list, and old tests. Study guides have information about areas of emphasis and some have practice questions. Sometimes study guide questions or similar questions appear on tests. So I work these out in advance. The syllabus is one of the student's best friends because it shows what is going to happen and when it is going to happen. It shows us when the troops will arrive and from what direction. We can be in the right place when they do. The syllabus shows each stage and how each fits into the course. Some professors have their own lecture notes (typed or untyped) or handouts, which they are glad to give to interested students in advance. Old tests and old papers are often found in the department library, with the department secretary, with previous students or with the professor himself. Old tests and old papers show the style of questioning, degree of difficulty, types of issues that come up, and other elements that the professor tends to emphasize. This is a reliable tool because most professors don't change their test questions or style much over time. There are many reasons for this. One is that the basic principles and take home messages of the class don't change much in the course of a few years. Another reason is that a particular type or line of questioning might create a consistent curve for the course. There are also issues of time and convenience. Professors are very busy with research and other responsibilities. Some feel that it is too inconvenient to come up with completely fresh questions. Sometimes they only change a few numbers or other small details. Some take questions from the back of chapters or the back of their favorite textbooks. Some students even ask the professor about his favorite books on the topic; then the students study questions in these books (even if these books are not assigned)."

Establishing a Rapport: "I also meet with the professor before the quarter to establish a friendly rapport. When I introduce myself, I tell him why I am taking the course, my objectives, major, career goals, and life goals. I ask for advice on the things that I should look out for. The professor usually responds to my kindness by telling me about himself, his interests, research goals, and his other activities. I establish a connection, find common ground, and begin to develop a positive relationship before the lack of time of the academic term begins. This gets me off to a good start and sets the stage for future communications, appointments, meetings, conferences, and other interactions with the professor. Having a good relationship with the professor helps me to get excited about attending class, the subject, and the course."

"Meeting with the professor before the course has unintended consequences," a student at the University of Oregon said. "One consequence is that it creates a strong first impression. The student is stigmatized in a positive way. Once someone is placed on the 'best student list,' it is difficult to be removed from it. Once someone arrives at a sincere judgment about someone else, they are generally reluctant to change their judgment, even in the face of new evidence. Teachers establish their biases about students early in the process. Another unintended consequence is that it establishes credibility. The person is taken as a serious student. In the future, if the student is academically on the borderline, the professor will give the student the benefit of the doubt and give the higher grade. If something outside of class takes place, the professor is more likely to believe that the excuse is legitimate." When you are on the borderline, the way and direction in which you fall makes a difference. It is also important to let the professor know in advance about any possible interference factors, as this will increase the chance that he will believe you and respond in an optimistic way, if something happens. "Definitely tell professors if you are on any sports teams or organizations that will cause you to miss class," a student at Hampton University said. "It is not asking for preferential treatment. It is being responsible. It shows that you are planning ahead and taking the course seriously." A student at Southern Arkansas University advised, "If you must miss a class, tell the instructor in advance and get the notes for that class from the instructor herself BEFORE the class. You'll have the best notes because they are coming directly from the instructor and she will think that you were wise for asking. Otherwise, get the notes from a student who tends to take comprehensive and legible notes. Tell that student in advance too. This will heighten the students awareness and increase the chance of getting the notes in good form." Perhaps a third unintended consequence has to do with comfort level. As a student at the University of Illinois remarked, "Even if a student has high numbers, some professors just don't feel comfortable about giving an A+ unless they have some kind of rapport with the student or know something about the student and the student's goals."

Some students start the main reading for their courses before the academic term begins. "I would meet the course instructors before the previous semester's classes ended, and ask them about the course text and ancillary materials, as well as suggested additional reading materials, often borrowing these materials from them for a couple of weeks so that I would not have to spend additional money on these books. During the holiday break before school started, I used my spare time to read the material, first just skimming through it as I would read a novel or an interesting magazine article, and then once again in some more depth. Before the course started, I had understood most of the material, knew exactly what I did not know, what else I needed to learn, and what questions to ask. I made an appointment with the instructor to get these questions answered offline. I was often way ahead of the rest of the class.

Courses were usually a breeze for me from then on! With just two to three weeks of hard work before the semester, I was able to enjoy myself during the semester. I was also able to focus on laboratory work and other projects which often are a major part of my grade!" "Read early and often," a student at Stanford University advised. "I read the first 30% of the book before the course starts so that I am ahead.... Then before each lecture, I reread the chapter to be covered."

4.8 Moving onto Campus Before the Academic Term

"I moved into my housing at the university a couple weeks earlier than I was expected to be there," a student at the University of Cincinnati reported. "I removed all distractions and added things in each room that facilitated the activity planned for that room. I added things that put me in a good state of mind. I put pictures of family members on the counter and pictures of people succeeding at something on the walls. I imagine succeeding with them or in their place. My study room is given no TV, radio, nor telephone. I use organizers so that everything has a home within a home and to extend the number of possibilities in a small space. I restrict each part of each organizer to one type of item and make sure that there is space for more of each item in its space."

"Get to the campus early!" a student at the University of Pennsylvania insisted. "The closer you get to the beginning of the semester, the more competition there is for the most basic things that you need and want. I go to places on campus before long lines form and get 'my choice' of books, guides, calendars, pens, paper, index cards, staplers, post-it notes, etc. I pick ones with colors that standout to make learning more exciting!"

"I look through each book to see what each contains. This was learned the hard way. In my first year, I went onto the campus to find resources for a major project. When I returned, I realized that the information was already in the appendix of the textbook on my desk in my apartment. Now, when I open a book, one of the first things that I do is go to the back of the book to see what extra information is hidden there. I ask myself, 'How can I take advantage of this information? How might I use it in the future?' In most cases, it gives me an advantage because most students in the class will never use the back of the book. So, I look through each book to see what it contains. I also look at the table of contents and think about how each section relates to each other. I gain a sense of the book's direction and why we are learning this material."

A student at the University of Washington also learned something from a bad experience. "At my first university," she stated, "I and others studied in the same few main places on campus even though they were less than ideal places to study. One day a friend of mine invited me to study with her in a cozy library on campus that I did not even know existed. I then began to question what I and other students really know about the university and what it has to offer beyond the basic areas where most people go. So I wandered into areas of the university where I usually don't go and I really learned a lot about what is available. Some of it is not publicized but it is there for use. This is also true for many things in life; it may not be publicized but it is there for use. At my next university, I deliberately went there well before the semester started and took an official tour of the campus. I wandered into unpopular areas to discover neat unpublicized study places and services for students. Then I knew where to go for a service or a great place to study and could go directly there without wasting time or depending on places that are popular but not ideal for me."

4.9 Priority Lists

A student at the University of Florida said, "Before school begins, the student should prioritize activities for the coming term. Write down a list of possible activities, and rank them. If you have seven things listed and can handle four of them effectively on a regular basis, then only sign up for the four. If one is borderline, remove it from your list and have a tight package. My motto is, 'If you cannot do it effectively on a regular basis, then don't sign up for it.' Irregular effectiveness rarely leads to something meaningful. One of the biggest mistakes is for students to overload themselves with commitments from the beginning." Another student, at Green River Community College, explained, "I strike a balance between people and studies. Studies usually outweigh people by an 80 to 20 ratio. So I apply this ratio to the time that I have available outside of class." Some students also decide the proportion of time they will spend on each class relative to their other classes. Some prioritize the time for each class based on level of importance of the class. There are different criteria of importance. These include: the level of difficulty; amount of time or effort required; impact on grade point average; impact on major; and impact on getting into a specialized school. Some students use these criteria to prioritize individual assignments within classes too. Other criteria include the order of allocation of the assignments by the instructor and the assignment due date. Time is distributed proportionally according to the chosen criteria. For example, at the level of individual assignments, a student at Rutgers University used impact on grade. One assignment in his class was worth 30% of his grade and the other was worth 70%. So he distributed the time that he made available outside of lecture to study for this class, according to this 30 to 70 ratio.

4.10 Accomplishing Individual Goals

An effective way to accomplish a goal is to break it down into manageable pieces and then address one piece at a time. A student at the University of Pennsylvania explained eight steps. One: define what needs to get done as a goal. Two: write this goal down on paper. Three: break the goal down into smaller manageable pieces. If a piece is still large, break it into smaller pieces until it feels comfortable. Four: define a chronological order for these pieces. This can be based on a natural order of events, degree of importance, degree of difficulty, degree of comfort, or personal preference. Each piece is now a step in a sequence towards the final goal.

Five: add quality-control steps to the sequence. Quality-control steps can include reminders, previews, drafts, review of work by self, review by others, review with others, and a false deadline. An example of an early false deadline is one week before the actual deadline for the final goal. An early false deadline leaves room for such pitfalls as missed buses; broken alarm clocks; unavailable resources; steps that take longer than expected; bad advice; misdirection; incorrect or incomplete instructions; teachers who return drafts late, add things onto assignments at the last moment, are disorganized or insensitive; things that inevitably happen just before a deadline; and other unpredictable factors. An early false deadline heads the crisis off at the pass. It is a built-in protective mechanism. Some students get a grade that is lower than what the quality of their work deserves because they did not take into account and prepare for the reality of the unpredictable 30%.

Six: estimate how long it will take to accomplish each step in the sequence. Seven: assign a mini deadline (including time of day) to each step. Eight: write all deadlines (including mini deadlines, false deadlines, and actual deadlines) into a day planner.

"It seems trivial," a student at Harvard University said, "but one of the best things I ever did was use a day planner. It prevents unpleasant surprises and rushed work. At the beginning of the week, I outline any minor homework for the week and schedule it by day. My first year in college, I didn't use a planner, and I felt like I was just trying to survive day by day. Beginning sophomore year, I started using one almost religiously, and it revolutionized my academic life by giving me a plan of attack. I felt under pressure much less frequently since I always knew what was in store for each day, week, month, and so on. Lots of people have planners, but I don't feel that most realize just how useful a tool it is and so they under-use it, if at all." "There are way too many tasks involved with each class to try and remember them all," a student at the University of California at Berkeley claimed. "A daily planner keeps you from having to remember what you have to do, and allows you to focus on doing it." A student at Boston University pointed out, "There are a lot more hours in the day than most people realize and a planner helps you to use each one productively. You're organized and ready to get down to business. You recognize potential conflicts earlier than you otherwise would and still have time to do something about them."

Many of the students prefer a day planner to a calendar because day planners typically have more space reserved for each day and slots reserved for parts of each day; the student can place mini-deadlines for more than one goal on a page for a particular day and in specific time slots. As a result, many stages of several goals are integrated into one organized unit.

There are other things that students include in the daily planner. Some include warnings about how many days are left before an actual deadline. As a student at the University of Wyoming said, "I find that creative obscenities directed at myself in writing will generally catch my attention." Meetings, scheduled breaks, social events, and family events can be added. Some students use different colors for different types of events and deadlines. Examples are the use of the color red or highlight for actual deadlines. A student at Stanford University emphasized, "Remember, every single detail of one's life should not be included. That would be overwhelming. Have balance. Exclude regular events that are already engrained in your memory." "It is important to be realistic," a student at Michigan Technical University advised. "If you know that something doesn't work, don't put it in your planner. Some people write plans to do things that they know will not happen." "Follow your planning," a student at the University of Virginia said, "so that it is not done in vain!"

4.11 To Do Lists

Many of the participants also maintain a "To Do" list containing miscellaneous errands like checking email, dropping a letter off, or calling the cable man. In some cases, the list might include things that do not need to be broken down into smaller pieces, as well as some things that may not have immediate deadlines.

Some students simply write the title "To Do" at the top of a blank page and list items in outline form below it. Some prefer using a word processor, storing the list on a removable disk or computer for easy modification. A number of students rank the items in order of importance, placing a rank number next to each item. The student then begins accomplishing items on the list starting with the highest ranked item, moving one item at a time to the lowest ranked one. This way, the most important things get done first. "Each time I accomplish something on my To Do list, I cross it out and feel good about myself," a student at the University of Illinois at Urbana-Champaign said. As more things are added to the To Do list over time, the student can briefly re-rank the list, cross out the old rank numbers, write in new rank numbers, and again begin the process of accomplishing from the highest ranked item. Each time the person has a bit of spare time (for example, fifteen minutes here or there), he can address the next item on the list. The person takes advantage of the accumulation of little pockets of time that exist throughout the day.

There are various types of To Do lists. Some contain categories. One example is a To Do list that has a "Before 5 PM" category and an "After 5 PM" category. In many places, services, departments, and businesses close by 5 PM. Things that need to be done before 5 PM are placed in the "Before 5 PM" category. Things that can wait until after 5 PM or need to be done after 5 PM are placed in the "After 5 PM" category. The cut-off time or threshold does not have to be 5 PM; it can be any time that is appropriate for the person's location or situation. Another form of To Do list has categories depicting level of importance. Some use categories like "Important" and "Very Important" or "Don't Forget" and "Definitely Don't Forget." Another example is a list with the categories "1," "2," and "3," where "1" is the most important category and "3" is the least important.

4.12 Binders

"I assign a binder to each class," a student at the University of Minnesota at Duluth explained. "The first division in each binder is a planning section. The planning section contains priority lists, class schedule, revision timetable, and outlines or flow charts of how I will do major assignments. The other labeled divisions in each binder are the following: reading notes; lecture notes; questions; corrections; journal; grade sheets; vocabulary; homework; post-assignment comments; post-test comments; miscellaneous; and extra paper. I have a division for every issue so that I know where everything is and can go directly there. The issues are separated, and things don't get lost. I have extra dividers and binder pockets in the back of each binder so that I can adjust to changes as they take place. Sometimes, these changes even take place in class."

One of the divisions mentioned by the student at the University of Minnesota is for grade sheets. Many participants noted that they use grade sheets. For example, a student at the University of South Dakota explained that she tallied points as she moved through each course. Her grade sheet contained a running total of her grade and current percentage in the course. She used the sheet to re-prioritize her use of time during the term, as situations and her standings in her courses varied. She also used it to address differences with teachers. "If you ever have a discrepancy with a professor on what he or she believes your grade is, compared to what you believe your grade is," she said, "you have everything itemized on paper. This has saved me more than one time. Professors ARE human and do make mistakes." Grade sheets also motivate some students to do well because they want to see high numbers on their own grade sheets.

4.13 You Can Do It

Many participants described the importance of not accepting negative language like "I'll probably just get a B," "I'm not good at math," "They're smarter than me," or "They know more than I do." Some of the advice from participants included the following: "The individual's mindset when going into a course is most of the battle"; "There are no limitations, only the ones that you think exist"; "You are what you believe you are"; "Academics is all about thinking that you can!"; "You have the mentality for it"; "You have to realize that you can do anything"; "If you believe it, you can achieve it"; "You just make a commitment, and accept nothing less."

One student at the University of Wisconsin-Eau Claire told herself that it was possible not only to do well but also to be one of the best at whatever she set her mind to. She stated that her attitude was good for her spirits and made her work harder. Last year she took an honors physics class. She had never taken a physics class before. She imagined herself succeeding, studied for the class consistently every night, met with study partners to go over homework, and bothered her professor with questions almost every time he had office hours. She worked the hardest she had ever worked for a class before and was rewarded with one of the top scores in the honors physics class.... It began with a belief in herself. A student at Columbia University said, "I tell myself that I am willing to be the best. I am willing to do what is necessary to be number one." A student at the University of California at Berkeley stated, "Make a promise to yourself to be the best that you can be, and don't break the promise!"

SECTION 5: BEGINNING OF THE ACADEMIC TERM

Some students described the importance of starting things early in the academic term. "At the beginning of each semester," a student at Central Michigan University explained, "I look through the syllabus for deadlines and test dates; I consider the pathways I will take as well as preliminary review and final review dates for each. Then, I start plugging away, right away. I think of what things I can do now to clear the paths and to reduce the stress that is expected around the time of these deadlines. If there is something I can do now, I do it now." A student at North Carolina State University at Raleigh said, "Our college offers 'makeups' if two exams are scheduled on the same day. So just avail yourself of the policy or ask a professor as soon as you notice the tight schedule." Other responses included the following: "'DO IT NOW!!!' because even though it seems that there is plenty of time, Murphy's law will get you!"; "Do it so that when things go wrong, it is already done"; "Get up earlier than others in your house, look outside, and 'feel what it feels' to be ahead of the rest of the world. Then get down to business"; "Start early, and bug every legal reference you can"; "Keep an eye on the schedule and keep thinking ahead; while waiting for more information on one assignment, get a 'good start' on another assignment. Work hard to get 100's on the first quizzes, examinations, midterms, and assignments because the material only becomes more complex and the tests get harder as the course progresses"; "Regularly do a little more than you are required to do."

A student at Yale University said, "I use a reverse two-week strategy. I treat the first two weeks in the same way that most people treat the last two weeks. In the first two weeks of the term, I cram like it is finals. I make sure that by the end of the second week, I am two chapters ahead in each of my classes. At this two-week point, I simply study at the same pace as the class. This cycle keeps me ahead for the rest of the term.

The feeling of being ahead of the class is a thrill and it is easy to enjoy studying when I am there. I can handle problems that come up too."

"The two week point is critical because where students are at this point is often where they remain for the rest of the term. Some people relax in the first two weeks and find themselves a chapter behind. They read the chapter, thinking that they are okay, and find that the class has moved ahead to the next chapter. Now, they are again a chapter behind. They read the next chapter and realize that the class has moved to yet another chapter. This cycle of being a chapter behind continues through the course; the person crams in the last two weeks, gets overwhelmed, and receives a low grade. How did the cycle get started? It was the activity of the first two weeks that set the pattern for the rest of the term. This is why I believe that the first two weeks are the most important weeks in the term. Students should target this window of time."

"Sometimes quiz questions are straight out of the homework due later that week or the next chapter of the book," a student at Stanford University disclosed. "If you have already read the chapter and how to combine the information, you will be prepared for these quizzes." An anonymous student said, "When I took Spanish, our weekly vocabulary quizzes included some words that were scheduled to be taught that day or the next day. Putting things from the future on the current quiz is a bit unfair but it is not uncommon for instructors to do this in school." A student at Columbia University stated, "Sometimes you have to send off for articles in journals to support your papers. It can take a while for the journal articles to arrive in the mail. So you need to send off for them early." "A crucial part of starting early," a student at North Carolina State University explained, "is that people are generally slow to respond. Schedules bottleneck at school. At the last minute, professor and assistant help are too busy to spend much time on you; earlier in the term, they would have gladly taken an hour to unfold the entire answer before your eyes." A student at the University of Florida pointed out

"When you present a draft for a teacher to review, he will respond according to his schedule, not according to your schedule. Give it to him on time or late, and he will get it back to you late. Give it to him early, and he will get it back to you on time."

SECTION 6: BEFORE CLASS

6.1 When to Do Reading and Written Assignments

"Most students let the lecture be their first exposure," a student at the University of Colorado said. "Then they read the chapter that covers the lecture later in the day. A better habit is to read the chapter one day before the lecture that covers it. Do this everyday for all of your classes. This strategy will keep you at the top of your classes. Reading the corresponding chapter one day before the lecture means that you will be able to squeeze more out of the lecture and take full advantage of what the lecture has to offer. You'll come into the lecture with a solid frame of reference and feeling good about yourself. You will more effectively grasp concepts; recognize subtleties that others are missing or misinterpret; fill in missing links; pin-point both details that need clarification and differences between the lecture and the book; write better notes; follow fast moving and complex lectures; and follow professors who cut the lecture short, speak softly, skip critical pieces of information, are unclear or otherwise poor presenters. You will be ready for surprise quizzes. You will be better prepared for your own deficits, deficits in the teacher, and in the process or system. You will have more intelligent questions, which will gain the respect of your teacher and fellow classmates. I knew that I had gained the respect of at least one classmate when he said, 'If you know this stuff, why are you taking the course?' On top of this, the information simply sinks in better this way, and for longer."

A student at Stanford University stated, "Some instructors give both the reading and written assignments in advance. For example, the syllabus might state that the reading assignment that corresponds to tomorrow's class is chapter 4, and the accompanying written assignment will include problem numbers 3, 7, 10, 12, and 19 in the back of chapter 4. Do BOTH the assigned reading and the problem set the day before the class." A student at Clemson University explained, "I do my homework problems right after doing the reading. This is because when I apply what I learn to something immediately after learning it, I am able to retain the information for longer."

6.2 Environment

Some students described the significance of reading environment. "The best reading strategy that I can offer is to be in 'your own little corner, in your own little chair' (like Cinderella)..." a student at Hampton University said. "It's amazing how the chapters fly when one is comfortable and in her own space." A student at Columbia University likes to study in a quiet secluded corner in his room. Another student, at the University of California at Berkeley, remarked, "I look forward to reading when I know that my friends and I are going to spend the day in Tilden Park (a national park in the Bay Area) and bring food and blankets. Lucky for me, I always get my reading finished this way. I have yet to do all of my assigned reading sitting at home with the phone, computer, guitar, friends, etc." A student at the University of Michigan pointed out that he studies best at a table with a friend who is studying a different subject. He benefits from the person's company and is able to read his subject at his own pace. A student at the University of Oregon studies in a coffee shop. He likes the pleasant atmosphere, the background sound, the presence of other people, and the knowledge that he can have a snack or coffee while he finds his way through the work. A student at Stanford University likes to change his study environment every three or four hours. The new environment is refreshing.

"Consider different kinds of sound," a student at Rutgers University said. "You might find a particular type of sound that facilitates your study." I personally like to study with inspirational jazz music that does not include lyrics. The inspirational elements of the music keep me motivated. Since this music does not contain lyrics, there are no words to interfere with my thoughts as I read. Some of the musicians who play this kind of music include David Benoit, Dave Koz, Marc Antoine, and Ottmar Liebert.

Students can also experiment with different volumes of sound for their study environment. A student at Hampton University remarked that her roommate's favorite place to study is on a couch in their "loud, semi-chaotic lobby." Different sounds and volumes are best for different individuals.

One change in environment that made a difference for some students is a brighter bulb. A change from 60 Watts to 100 Watts can be dramatic. It also makes a difference to direct the light towards the page. Other changes include a better chair, a different posture (e.g. upright), and different colors. "In some western societies," a student at the University of Maine said, "the colors white, yellow, blue, and green are thought to be refreshing. Bright colors are thought to be energetic and modern. Yellow is associated with happiness and energy. Pink is soothing and affectionate. Orange is linked with happiness and provokes conversation and appetite. Orange-yellows, peaches, tans, browns, and reds are associated with coziness and warmth. Tans, beige, and grays are restful. Blues and greens are cool and calm. Purple is linked with comfort but it is also linked with mystery. Red is associated with passion and power. Black is linked with power, authority, independence, and discipline." The student can consider the influence of colors in her environment, including the colors of utensils and other materials used for school.

One student at the University of Pennsylvania found that a change in her attitude towards her environment made a difference. She took long bus rides and realized that she could take advantage of this long period to read while on the bus. She completed additional reading and was proud of her mental ability to adjust to her environment.

A student at Columbia University said, "Students can train themselves to focus in any environment. Try the following technique: In a quiet room, pick an object and ask questions about its details. What color is it? What is its size? What are its components? How large are the grains relative to each other, and in what direction do the grains move? Questions force you to focus on the object. Next, try this exercise in an environment where there is a slight distraction. With practice, you will be able to focus despite the presence of the slight distraction. Next, practice in an environment where there is a big distraction (like loud music). Soon, you will be able to focus in any environment."

6.3 How They Read and Take Notes Before Class

6.3.1 Reading

Some of the participants described how they read. "First," a student at Carnegie Mellon University explained, "I decide what I will read, why I am reading this, and what my reading objectives are. Next, I read and scrutinize any of the following things that exist: Front cover, back cover, preface, about the author, table of contents, titles, subtitles, headings, subheadings, introduction, tables, charts, diagrams, conclusion and summary. This creates ordered categories in my mind so that my brain knows where to store each detail. My third step is to predict what will be in each category so that I can compare this with what I actually find when I do the reading. Next, I read all of the way through the reading quickly for general concepts and to identify which parts are more important than others. Then I read all of the way through a second time for 'detail.' This second reading entails reading fast for those areas that were deemed to be less important during the first reading, and reading slow for those areas that were deemed to be more important. The notes that I take during this second reading follow the same pattern: I write fewer notes for those areas that were deemed to be less important, and more notes for those areas that were deemed to be more important; usually less than 30% of the reading is really important."

The idea of reading once for concepts and a second time for detail was a common suggestion. A student at Cambridge University said, "I was told once that in an examination you need to show the examiner the surface of the cake for breadth and a slice of the cake for depth. You can do the same in reading. Skimming through once to have an idea of the structure and overall direction gives the surface layer. The detailed reading and note taking of particular parts gives you some depth."

Many students actively ask questions during their second reading. "As I read the second time," a student at the University of Virginia remarked, "I think critically about what I am reading. This keeps me alert and makes the reading more exciting. Don't be intimidated by the author's credentials. Pretend that it is your job to catch the author's shortfalls and to highlight them. Pretend that you are an investigator trying to see if this person and his writing really checks out. Act as if you are the most curious person in the world about this. What assumptions, biases, or speculations does this author exhibit? Are there points that the author has de-emphasized, concealed, or forgotten? Did the author adequately achieve the objectives described in the introduction? Did he present adequate evidence to support his claims? What do you want to know about the subject? Is he giving you the information that you need? What question did the author really address? What did the author really accomplish? In what ways could he have done a better job in his research, interpretation, or presentation? In what ways could the author have related this to other relevant information? At each step, ask yourself if you are really convinced."

Other responses included the following: "Make it a goal to gain at least two pieces of information from every major paragraph"; "Think about how the information might help all of us to better understand the past, the present, or the future. How might it affect unresolved issues? What implication does this have for our future? What is the next reasonable step in the author's work? What concepts, assumptions, and limitations lye behind the formulas?"; "Ask 'how' and 'why' for everything"; "Keep yourself oriented with the five power items, who, what, where, when, and how?"; "What are the definitions and limitations of each item?"; "What would happen if we were to change (decrease, increase, or remove) one element of the equation?"; "Why should we care about this or even believe this author?"; "You don't have to answer all of your questions but the fact that you took the time to ask these questions puts you ahead of other students." A student at the University of Oregon said, "Determine the basic relationships, directions, and messages that each chart, table, and graph in the reading depicts."

"Remember the five natural senses," a student at the Massachusetts Institute of Technology advised. "These are sight, hearing, smell, touch, and taste. For critical information that must be recalled at a later point, make a mental note of what you experienced on each of these five senses at the time that you read this critical information. Also make a mental note of the place, mood, and time that you are learning it. Think about where you see it on the page. Think about the temperature, what is in your immediate environment, and what actions or movements are taking place at the time. In the future, if you are stuck on an examination and you are having trouble remembering something, you can recall it by thinking of the senses that you experienced at the time you originally learned it."

"After reading a section," a student at Stanford University advised, "I stop and quiz myself. I ask, 'What were the main points of this section? What details were particularly important? What questions would I expect to see on an examination?'" One student at the University of Washington goes to the table of contents and quizzes himself from there.

Some students described taking notes in outline form during their second reading. One way to write in outline format is to start each subsequent subcategory one indentation to the right on the page. An additional option (though less popular) is to add Roman numerals, capital letters, Arabic numerals, and lower-case letters, in series with each move to the right of the paper. Some students write and underline a title for each category and subcategory of the outline; the headings and subheadings in the text can be used for this or the student can create his own. Some students place keywords in the margins of the notes to remind them of what that section of the notes is about. The mind remembers information well when it is labeled. Other suggestions for the outlined notes were the following: "Each time, before you write something, ask yourself if writing this item is consistent with your purpose for reading this material"; "Write less for those parts that were found to be less important during your first reading and more for those parts that were found to be more important"; "Include all bold and italicized words from the text"; "Use your own words to make the notes more meaningful to you"; "Include any of your own thoughts and important questions"; "Where possible, deliberately minimize the number of words that you write"; "Use fragments of sentences, bullet points, hyphens, commas, semicolons, and colons to make the notes succinct"; "Use simple pictures, lines, or arrows"; "Look-up and write the definitions of words you don't know"; "Source the information in your outline." "Incorporate spaces between sections to leave open the option of adding additional comments, questions, thoughts and notes later."

I mentioned above that many students do the reading twice: They read all of the way through once quickly to determine structure and determine what is important. They read through a second time with curious questions and an increased focus on those important areas. They write minimized notes in outline form with a focus on important areas; they write more notes for the important areas and fewer notes for the less important areas. However, another popular approach was to read only once but with the curious questions. As he reads, the student makes predictions about what comes next. The student does not take notes word-for-word or line-by-line. Instead, he reads one or two paragraphs ahead before writing notes, and then distills on paper in outline form the few things that are important in those one or two paragraphs. The student continues to the end, reading with curious questions, making predictions, and stopping every one or two paragraphs to distill the newest important information into the notes.

There are many benefits to the outline format. It results in a clear organization of ideas, keeps the student mindful of overall structure, reduces clutter, and makes notes easy to read, understand, and reference at a later point in time. A student at Brown University said that the outline format forces him to paraphrase in his own words; this process reinforces the ideas in his mind.

Once these notes are written, the student does not have to return to the text at a later point in time! The important information has been distilled and translated into the student's own language in an organized way. This saves time and stress in the future!

A student at the University of Saint Thomas at Houston acknowledged, "If the book reads like a radio manual, instead of writing an outline, I simply jot down summaries of each section as I read." A student at Harvard University stated, "For some courses with heavy reading (say, five-hundred or more pages a week), I favor giving most of the required reading a cursory read, not worrying about every single last detail. Then I focus on the details given in the lecture."

A small percentage of the participants suggested ideas that entailed a continued relationship with the reading. These ideas included marking concerns at their points, highlighting, and underlining.

Marking Concerns at Their Points: Some participants believe in writing questions, answers, and/or comments directly in the textbook (if the student owns it) or on a post-it tab at the locations where the problems exists. The student can resolve the issue at a future point in time at the specific site of the problem. For some students, this helps the answer to sink in better because the student can think of the site where she saw it in the reading; the point is then reinforced. Pinpointing the location in the reading where the problem exists also helps the instructor to learn the context of the student's question and do a more effective job of answering it. One student had a practice of placing post-it notes at critical points in the reading irrespective of whether or not she had questions at those locations.

Highlighting: A student at Brown University insisted that "Highlighting during the first reading is deadly since you may highlight things which are not as important and completely miss things which are. If you are going to use highlighting, I suggest that you wait until the second reading to begin highlighting so that it is placed in the right places. Some students highlight too much; when it comes time for the test, they are essentially reading the whole thing over again." A student at Elmhurst College suggested that the student focus on only highlighting main ideas and main points in the reading so that too much is not highlighted. He said, "With this, all of the salient information will be available right before you in one quick reading when it is time to review for the examination." An alternative is to only do the reading once. The student reads one or two paragraphs ahead at a time before stopping and deciding which critical information in the two paragraphs will be highlighted.

A student at Embry-Riddle Aeronautical University uses three different highlight colors. He highlights all definitions in one color, all mathematical formulas in a second color, and all other important information in a third color. Another student, at Princeton University, uses three different colors to depict different levels of importance. Before a test, he at least re-reads the parts covered by the most important color.

"Before the lecture," a student at the University of Maine explained, "I highlight what I think is important in yellow. After the lecture, I go back and highlight in blue the things in the book that were covered in the lecture. Yellow and blue make green! Everything in green will definitely be on the test; at minimum, I learn what is in green before the test. Sometimes, I take notes on the stuff in yellow that falls just before or just after what is in green because sometimes the lecture only touches the surface of what you are expected to know."

Some students underline rather than highlight the text. Some students underline with pencil or pen. Some underline with colored pens. A student at Louisiana State University said, "Using colored pens helps me to make use of my visual senses to remember the information." The same techniques used for highlighting can be used for underlining. Some students only underline two types of words in important areas: (1) key words, and (2) connecting words (like "less than," "but," "and," and "or"); this can be helpful because these connecting words depict the context of the key words. These few words are underlined and reviewed by the student before the test(s).

6.4 Other Material to Be Covered Before Class

A student at Stanford University asserted, "My standard is to do the required reading plus at least 'one' additional thing, even if it is small. This way, I don't read too much but I cover more than other students do. It also gives me a certain confident feeling that I know more." A student at the University of Oregon said, "I identify one extra source (preferably in the library) for each of my courses." A student at the University of California at Los Angeles divulged that some students find out their professor's favorite text, and use this as the additional reading source.

A student at Harvard University said, "Instructors often assign optional reading. I do the optional reading religiously." A student at Rutgers University stated, "Sometimes, there is not enough time to read everything and the optional reading is known to be less important anyway. So, I 'get surgical' about the optional reading. I'll only read, for example, the introduction and conclusion of each of the optional readings to learn their main ideas or arguments. The point is to be systematic in how the optional reading is done. You don't have to read all of it—Just get to the main points that the optional reading has to offer." A student at the University of California at Los Angeles stated, "Since most students will not do the optional reading, doing any part of it means an advantage."

There were five other suggestions for things that can be done in addition to the required work:

1) Read literature referenced in the required reading.

2) Read other publications by the same author, a similar author, or one with an opposing point of view. Read publications that critique the author, the reading, or the subject. This publication might be an article in a journal, magazine, or newspaper. It can be a passage in a summary guide, an entire summary guide, a chapter in a book or an entire book. Students can find these publications by searching a citation, periodical, bibliographical, or book review index which covers the field. She can search a database on a school or library computer, the Internet, or a card catalogue in the library. She can browse for the subject in a local, on-campus, or online bookstore. Some online sources are listed in Appendix B.

Summary guides include Cliffs Notes, Barron's Book Notes, Max Notes, Monarch Notes, and Schaum's Outlines. A student at Central Michigan University pointed out that "These notes are cheap and only take a few minutes to read. Someone has already spent tens of hours that you don't have critiquing this in a professional way. So go ahead and make use of them. I have downloaded some of these for free at pinkmonkey.com. It's fair to use anything that is publicly available!"

3) Use a lecture note service: Some schools have a lecture note service; graduate students are paid to take lecture notes, type them, and make them available. One example of this is the Black Lightning lecture note service at the University of California at Berkeley. The typed notes for the current year and/or the years that the service has been available are made available to students who sign up and pay for the service. Some students like to read notes of this service corresponding to the previous year's lecture on the topic before each lecture.

4) Participate in online newsgroups or discussion groups on the topic, like those available through Usenet, kovacs.com/directory/, or bookspot.com/discussion.

5) Do additional problems. A student at Columbia University tries to do the five hardest questions in the back of the chapter before he starts the assigned homework problem set. The knowledge he gains from learning how to do these five hardest questions increases the chance that he will get all of the homework problems right, and that he will get the hardest problems on the examination right, as well.

6.5 Other Actions Before Class

(A) Talk to Others: A student at Stevens Institute of Technology said, "I like to talk to classmates about the reading in order to pick up interesting tidbits that I might have missed or unique perspectives that they may have to offer."

(B) Sleep: "I find sleep as one of the most critical instruments in optimizing one's experience in the classroom," a student at Harvard University declared. "There are diminishing marginal returns for staying up too late if you will not be able to participate effectively in class because you are too sleepy." Sleep can affect many things including ability to concentrate, think clearly, learn, and remember. One strategy is to decide an ideal sleep time and an ideal wake time in advance. Then force yourself to sleep and wake at those exact times everyday (with an alarm clock). Overtime, the body can adjust to the regularity of the schedule, automatically feel tired at the designated sleep time, and automatically wake at the designated wake time.

(C) Review: "Before class I re-read the notes I took in the previous class meeting to make sure I understood everything taught in that class," a student at the University of Cincinnati said. "If I find a topic that is unclear, I draw a star next to it and ask the professor for clarification when class begins. This process also helps me to connect what I learned in the last lecture with the present lecture."

(D) On the Way to Class: "I crank my walkman while walking to class," a student at City College of New York said. "The songs that I listen to are very specific in that they have to be motivational (like the song called 'War' by the band, U2). I go into a lecture prepared to do battle. I tell myself that I will learn this subject, will not allow myself to drift, will focus, ask questions, and understand the subject matter fully." There were two other suggestions. One was to look forward to each class as a new learning experience. The other suggestion was to visualize success. Imagine yourself smiling, taking notes, and listening successfully. Imagine the best outcome of events before they happen.

SECTION 7: DURING CLASS

7.1 Attend Class

"Attend class consistently," a student at the University of Pennsylvania advised. "At least 15% of what you need to know is in class and not in the textbook. There are extra details in class that you cannot afford to miss. These details have a way of showing up on examinations." It is also the case that attendance in class is a criterion for judgment.

Some students suggested showing up to class early. Comments from students included the following: "Arrive before the professor arrives and leave after the professor leaves"; "Being the first one to arrive and the last one to leave shows the instructor that you are there to learn, not just to PASS"; "Important announcements and summaries are often made just before the lecture or just after the lecture. You want to be there for these. If you depend on others, they might forget to tell you, only give you some of what was said or a modification of what was said."

Another suggestion was to sit in the front of the class. Observations from students included the following: "The people sitting in the first three rows get the best grades"; "In the front of the class you eliminate distractions, which for the most part are individuals who do not want to be in the class. If these people are out of sight, they are out of mind, and you won't be distracted by them"; "It is helpful to sit in the front of the lecture hall, preferably near the center. It is much harder to daydream or to nod off when you are right in front of the professor"; "When the only person in front of you is the instructor, it is as if he is teaching just to you"; "The teacher is more likely to remember your face at grading time if you sit in the front of the class on a regular basis."

"In the first week of class," a student at the University of Oregon advised, "take the initiative to introduce yourself to students sitting next to you. This is the time that people are most receptive to meeting someone new and exchanging contact information. Later in the course, students conveniently fall into what are sometimes unintentionally closed clicks; at the later point, it can be more difficult to initiate relationships as people are busier and settled in their ways."

"There are times in a course when you need to talk to someone in your class about some small detail, no matter how good you are. Students sitting in the front of the class with you tend to be serious students. It is good to build connections with them for academics and for meaningful relationships that make life and school more fun."

"When meeting someone new," a student at Kansas State University said, "associate his or her name with something that is significant to you, reminds you of someone famous, or a funny story. Use whatever hints you can create to help you remember it. For example, I met a girl named Reagan and I remembered her name because I associated it with the former President, Ronald Reagan. If the person's name is David Gill, you might associate it with the biblical story of David and Goliath or a fish named David who has 'gills.'" A student at the Massachusetts Institute of Technology said, "To remember a last name like 'Greenspun' you might picture that person with green hair. The next time you see him, you'll remember the image of him with green hair and recall his name." A student at Columbia University declared, "The mind is engineered to deal with images. Attach a simple clear image to the sound of each syllable or word in the person's name and you won't forget it. You can create a simple silly story with these images to further consolidate your memory of the person's name." A student at the University of Illinois at Urbana-Champaign repeats the person's name back at the person in the next sentence to help him remember the person's name.

On the first day of class, a student at Princeton University writes the title "Class Directory" on a blank sheet and a message for the sheet to be returned to him. He passes the sheet down the row to the others in the class. After class, he retrieves the sheet and makes a copy of this newly created class directory for himself and/or for the rest of the class. He uses the department's photocopy machine for free, has the department secretary photocopy it, or does it on his own means. He brings the copies of the class directory to the next class for himself and the other students. From that point on, he has a way to contact everyone in the class.

7.2 Before the Lecture Begins

"In class," a student at the University of California at Los Angeles said, "be prepared with materials. This should be obvious but some students are totally unprepared when coming to class. Have plenty of paper and pens out so that you aren't fishing in your bag while the professor is lecturing." A student at Texas Agricultural and Mechanical University said, "I have my note-taking materials (pen, paper) ready before the professor enters the classroom." A student at Columbia University advised, "Bring your textbook to class in case the instructor makes reference to it. Further, sometimes there are mistakes in the book that can be corrected right away."

"If there is time," a student at the University of Nevada at Reno stated, "I approach the lecturer with questions or issues that can be answered quickly. Too often we sit idly waiting for a lecture to begin. I take a few minutes to review the previous lecture notes. Constant review is yet another powerful tool."

7.3 Beginning of Lecture

Students offered suggestions for lecture. These included the following: "Don't slouch in your chair or fall asleep. Sitting up in the chair will reduce the chance of you falling asleep"; "Clear the mind of all other wandering thoughts"; "Pay attention. If your mind is not in the game, you can't catch the ball"; "Have a piece of gum or mints on hand to perk up your nervous system at certain points in the lecture"; "Pretend that this is the most interesting lecture in the world, and you are lucky to have a ticket to sit in on it"; "Pretend that this is the only exposure you will have to the material and you must get it now"; "Treat each word as if it is made of gold"; "Think of the words in terms of images and pictures"; "Look at the instructor's face and pretend that you are having an interesting conversation with him and no one else is around"; "Anticipate what the instructor will say next before actually hearing it. This stimulates the brain and keeps it active." "Evaluate how much you think you already know about a topic"; "Ask yourself about each piece of information: Do I remember reading about this? Did I understand it then? If not, what am I learning from the teacher now that enables me to understand it? What questions can I ask to clear it up? "; "Ask yourself if you could explain what you just heard to someone else." "Think of the topic as it exists in real life. Picturing osmosis taking place brings new meaning to the words which describe it"; "If the lecture is about management, think about yourself as a manager. What actions would you take as a manager?"; "If Newton's Law of Gravitation is being taught, think the way Newton must have been thinking at that time"; "Remind yourself at various points in the lecture of the day's topic to keep the main idea in mind"; "Ask yourself 'why' you are listening and what you are listening for"; "Be an active seeker of knowledge instead of a passive recipient of it"; "Participate actively and genuinely care about what the teacher and other students say and do. This will open you to a world of learning. If an in-class exercise is given, take full opportunity to exercise your knowledge. You might find that you will remember things and understand them much more clearly when you apply them in intellectual exercises. Raise your hand at least once a session and answer every question as best you can. If you are sure you understand something that another student finds confusing, try to help him or her. When you participate earnestly it makes school and life more interesting"; "In each class, ask yourself, 'What is my potential as a human being in this limited space of time? How can I expand my knowledge, skills or experience in any way? What component of this would I like to know more about? What elements of this can I do something with right now?'"

Further responses from students included the following: "If you don't speak up in class, some people, including some teachers will assume that you are not interested or that you don't know the material"; "Don't be too shy to ask questions. I have never seen a professor turn down a reasonable question—'reasonable' being anything having to do with the subject"; "Teachers know that their best students ask curious questions, just as the best experts in the field ask curious questions"; "Ask questions until you completely understand it. You won't have time to ask later"; "Ask questions as soon as you start to get lost. That way you don't let anything slip by you, and the issue does not come back to haunt you later"; "Ask the professor to give you one or more specific analogy or example to increase the standard of your understanding"; "Ask questions that tie the loose ends of the topic. You might find one or two of these in each class session."

7.4 Respect for the Teacher

Some students highlighted the importance of showing respect for the teacher. These responses included the following four comments: "I think my attitude and respect toward my teachers helped me because in return they were always very willing to help me out with questions"; "When you speak to a professor, make eye contact. Use a tone and content of communication that is respectful. One of the most important things to a professor is respect for his or her position"; "Some students use a tone that is disrespectful or politically incorrect, hinder the flow of instruction, or badger the teacher. This is what is called a 'problem child.' Problem children lose the goodwill of the professor and sometimes that of fellow students; once goodwill is gone, it is difficult to regain"; "If you appreciate the professor, let it show. Professors appreciate people who appreciate them and the materials that they have prepared. This is also true in the workplace. The boss appreciates employees who appreciate them, what they have put together, and the way they do things."

7.5 Taking Notes in Class

Many students described taking notes in class. One issue is paper. A student at Oxford University said that he prefers to use loose-leaf paper in class. It allows him to be more flexible. If information is taught or written in a bad order or if there are space-related problems, he can subsequently put things in the right order by re-arranging the loose-leaf paper and placing like information with like information. There were other suggestions for dealing with space-related problems. These included the following: "Take notes on half of the pages and leave the intervening pages blank"; "Leave spaces between sections as you write"; "Draw a line down the right side of the paper. Write your lecture notes on the left side of this line. Reserve the space on the right side of the line for questions, answers, comments, corrections, references, or additions from other sources."

Some students suggested labeling the notes. These suggestions included the following: "I adamantly place my name, class name, topic, day, date, and the page number in the upper right corner of the first page of my notes before the lecture begins. I write the page number and the date on the remaining pages. This is important because later it is easy for lecture papers to lose their order, lectures to lose their order, and to forget what days you missed part or all of the lecture. You cannot tell friends who might help what days you missed because you did not label your notes in the first place. These problems come to fruition at test time"; "The date is not significant now but it will become significant a month from now"; "Always date your notes. It puts everything in perspective and can actually stir your memory of certain subjects when you are reviewing for a test"; "Religiously write dates, ages, body counts, lovers, etc."

7.6 Lecture-note Format

Outline format is popular for both pre-lecture notes and lecture notes. The outline format offers the flexibility to write as little or as much as one chooses and still have a final product that is well organized. Some students use this format while writing every word that is spoken in class. Others use the outline format while writing short phrases or incomplete sentences. A common variation is to start class by writing every word that is spoken in outline format, and then deliberately switching to writing in short incomplete phrases while still in the outline format, if the lecture picks up pace.

As mentioned earlier, additional benefits of outline format are that it gets the point across effectively, reduces clutter, keeps the student mindful of overall structure, and lessens the chance of the student getting lost in the lecture's details. Later, when the student reviews the notes, they are easy to read, understand, and reference.

One student at Harvard University types her notes in class on a lab top computer. This makes it easy to re-arrange the information at the time or at a later point in time.

7.7 Amount to Write in Class

Many students argued the idea of diligently writing as much as possible of what is said in class and written on the board. Comments that supported this idea included the following: "It is better to have more than less of what you need"; "After class, you can change and remove information as appropriate"; "You might understand it at the time of the class but you might forget some of the details a month from now at test time"; "More details can mean more advantage"; "The lecture is the only time this information will be given in this way with these details"; "Writing everything helps some students to focus and keeps them alert."
There are other participants who believe in minimizing the amount of notes that they write in class. Some do not include details that are already permanently engrained in their minds, things that they've already written recently, or things that can be figured out quickly. "If the instructor uses the entire chalkboard to derive a formula," a student at Embry-Riddle Aeronautical University held, "I'll only copy the steps in the derivation that I wouldn't be able to find on my own. For example, I know that 2 + 2 = 4, so I wouldn't write that part." A student at Princeton University thinks hard about the true messages of the instructor's words at each step and only writes down in lecture what he perceives these messages to be.

Some students tailor the amount that they write in class to the professor's style. For example, a student at Rochester Institute of Technology explained that he writes fewer lecture notes if the instructor is one who tends to test on concepts or gives lots of credit for class participation. He writes detailed lecture notes if the instructor tends to test on specifics.

7.8 Color

A popular suggestion was the use of pens with retractable tips. The student can change the color of the ink by pushing a button on the pen which corresponds to the color of choice. One example of this is a four-color retractable pen with the colors black, blue, red, and green. Other suggestions included multifunction pens with retractable pen, pencil, and/or highlighter options. These options allow the student to quickly switch color and type of ink during lecture. Some students suggested the use of utensils with cushions to make long hours of writing comfortable. Some use colors to differentiate terms, definitions, ideas, concepts, people, and/or events as they write notes in class. Some use colors to distinguish levels of importance. For example, one student at Louisiana State University writes main points in one color and supporting points in another. Some people write notes from their reading before class in one color and add to those notes in a second color in class. Some feel that the use of color to make distinctions is organized, visually pleasing, and makes the information easier to retain. "If nothing else," a student at Cambridge University admitted, "colored pens make doodles more fun." Making it more fun, increases the chance of it getting done.

7.9 Other Distinctions

A student at Stanford University writes and underlines in his notes the term "Board" above information that was written on the board, "Spoken" above information that is spoken by the instructor, "Student" for useful points made by other students in class, and "Me" for his own thoughts and questions.

Some students mark areas of emphasis by highlighting them, either in their notes or directly in their textbook during the lecture. Some write comments directly in the textbook in class as they follow the lecture. Forms and handouts: Many students use handouts that are given in class as a basic structure but add notes in the available spaces and margins. Some people go the next step (particularly for long handouts) of making a distinction between the parts of the handout that are covered by the instructor and the parts of the handout that are not covered by the instructor in class. The student can write a minus sign next to each item (or the title of each section) that is not covered by the instructor in class. Alternatively, the student can write a plus sign next to each item (or the title of each section) that is covered by the instructor. A second approach is to draw a line down the left side of the paper next to parts of the handout that are not covered by the instructor in class. Alternatively, the student draws a line down the right side of the paper next to the parts of the handout that ARE covered by the instructor. If time runs out before an examination, the student can concentrate on knowing the parts of the handout that were actually covered in the lecture, and marked by these designations.

Some students use the handout as a guide with the option to refer to it later. They write notes separately in their notebooks. "While other students are dozing," a student at the University of Michigan at Dearborn suggested, "sharpen up your pencil and write! It sounds silly but it really does work." A student at Rutgers University said, "I take notes separately. It keeps me alert, allows me to cover everything that is important to the instructor in my own notebook, and avoids space-related problems that are common to handouts."

7.10 Shorthand

If the student doesn't know shorthand, there are other options. Mathematical symbols are great shorthand symbols to use because these are already engrained in many people's brains from early education.

Another option is abbreviation. One example is the use of the first three to five letters of the word or the word's consonants. Other options are acronyms, arrows to show steps in processes, simple flow charts, stick figures, and self-made symbols. The important thing is that it makes sense to you. A useful point is to decide in advance what each symbol will mean so that there is no confusion in class or at review time. If a symbol must be defined on the spur of the moment in lecture, one approach is to write the symbol and its definition before continuing. For example, "For the rest of this lecture, x = this, and y = that." Then continue writing notes with the new symbols, x and y, instead of using their time-consuming long forms. Another suggestion is to write lecture notes in your own vernacular without substituting for terminology that is important to the topic.

7.11 Speed

In addition to shorthand, there are other suggestions for dealing with speed-related issues in lecture. One is to draw an underline for the part of a sentence that is missed and continue writing the rest of the sentence. This maintains the context of the sentence. The student can return to fill-in the blank (right away or later). A similar approach is to write the second half of the sentence in its right place and then write the first half of the sentence in its right place.

Some students tape-record some lectures. They emphasize that they do not SOLELY tape-record the lecture. Instead, they take notes WHILE they tape-record the lecture. After the lecture, they listen to the tape and simply filled-in the missing parts in their notes. If this correction of the written notes is done on the same day, the same tape can be used for another day. One result is that the student does not have to buy a large number of tapes over time. Many only tape-record lectures on days when they are tired or predict that the lecture will move fast. One student at

Columbia University suggested buying a tape recorder that has a speed control option. One benefit is that the student can quickly get through less important parts and go slowly on more important parts.

"To increase the speed of your note taking ability," a student at Central Michigan University said, "practice writing the lyrics of songs you listen to for the first time on the radio. Don't use tapes; use the radio. You will be surprised one day how fast you can take notes without even looking at the paper. Trust me, it works. When I take notes of the lectures in my classes, I look at the instructor and I write in my notebook. I don't miss a single word the instructor says."

7.12 Slides

A student at the University of Minnesota said, "It is common for professors to cram a lot of information on slides and click through without providing the students enough time to write what is on each. The professor either plans improperly; misjudges or doesn't think about how long it takes students to write what is on each slide; or runs out of class time. Thus, if you see a professor setting up a projector at the beginning of class, approach him and ask if you can copy the slides after class for yourself or for the class. If not, wait until after his presentation, compliment him, and then ask if you can copy the slides. Take them to the division secretary and ask her to copy the slides for you or for the class (or do it yourself)." A student at Brunel University chooses a label for each slide and paraphrases what he perceives to be each slide's meaning, instead of writing everything on each slide. Another student, at Arizona State University, asks the instructor to slow down. Sometimes it works and sometimes it doesn't.

7.13 Study the Teacher

"Study what the teacher says in class," a student at the University of Cincinnati suggested, "but also study the teacher herself. Make note of times when she articulates words slowly, spends a disproportionate amount of time on a subject, repeats words, phrases, or issues, consciously or subconsciously emphasizes a point with body language, mannerism, emotion, or attitude. Note material that the teacher refers to or shows strong disagreement with, even if she does not cover it in class; these issues might become the surprise questions on tests. Emotionally positive or negative responses to comments or questions from students can also give information about the teacher's perspective. Interpret these as hints of importance and mark them as such."

7.14 Five Senses

A student at the Massachusetts Institute of technology claimed, "Some of the differences between students have to do with where they stand on each of the natural senses. For example, some people are hearing-oriented; they remember best by listening to themselves, other students, the instructor, or a tape recorder. Some are sight-oriented. They remember more of what they see. They might find it useful to see and use color pens, highlighters, post-its, written words, typed words, underline, pictures, figures, diagrams, flow charts, or mind maps. Some people are movement-oriented. They associate what they are learning with facial and other physical gestures. They might express themselves with gestures too. Some of them need to have their fingers moving with something, like a utensil or on a keyboard. Touch-oriented students also like to have their hands involved; examples include writing or constructing something. Taste-oriented people might find it useful to have gum or candy in their mouths. They might associate what they are learning with categories of food or the process of making food. Smell-oriented people associate what they are learning with a scent. The student can determine which sense is best for him and focus on learning techniques that use that sense. He might develop the senses that are weak, and/or use many senses at once.

7.15 End of Lecture

"Many students make the mistake of leaving five minutes before the lecture is over," a student at the University of Pennsylvania said. "The instructor usually has important points at the very end or provides a concise summary (the notes of which would be extremely helpful). So don't leave early." A student at Brown University suggested that "If you do not understand the day's lecture or have specific questions, corner the professor immediately upon the conclusion of the lecture and politely but persistently badger him or her until your questions are answered or you arrange a time to meet. At this time the information is still fresh in his (and your) mind and he may be better able to answer your question. Later, the instructor might forget what he said in class, how he said it, or why he said it. He might also have lost interest at that time."

"I also don't hesitate to compliment a professor or treat her like a friend," a student at the California Institute of Technology offered. "They are there to help us and typically respond well if we show our enthusiasm and appreciation." Another student, at the University of Pennsylvania, said, "After a lecture, I try to talk to someone about it on the way out of class. Having to articulate my reaction to the lecture helps crystallize the key points in my mind."

SECTION 8: AFTER CLASS

SECTION 8A: REWRITING THE NOTES

8A.1 General Concept and Benefits

A common pattern among the students surveyed was to rewrite lecture notes immediately or soon after the lecture. One anonymous student schedules her classes one hour apart so that she can rewrite her notes immediately after each lecture. A second example is a student at Columbia University who takes a twenty-minute break after class; then he reviews and rewrites his lecture notes. One benefit of rewriting the lecture notes soon after class on the same day is that the student can fix problems that inevitably exist in notes while the information is still fresh in his and in the instructor's mind. If the student waits, particularly for more subtle issues, he is more likely to forget what the issue was and what he was hoping to get from it. The instructor is also less likely to remember some details. A second benefit of rewriting the lecture notes soon after the class is that it sets the stage for the final review of notes before a test. Right before a test, there is not enough time to research questions or reinterpret the professor's language, scribbles, cut-off sentences, inaccuracies, or missing information for each lecture. The cumulative amount is beyond the scope of the time available just before a test. If the corrections and modifications are made on the day of the lecture, the student will easily glide through well cultivated notes, enjoying the nice colors, pictures, and smoothened language along the way at the time of the final review. A third benefit of rewriting the lecture notes on the same day is that it reinforces the material early, providing longer retention. If time runs out later, the student already knows it. Some students explained that they did well on tests not because of what they did last but rather because of early consolidation.

8A.2 How to Rewrite the Notes

The student can rewrite the notes by (1) correcting them; (2) merging them with notes on the topic that were taken before the lecture; (3) re-organizing the merged notes; and finally, (4) attaching mnemonics. This four-step process takes some time but this is the time to do it.

(1) Correct the Notes

The student corrects the lecture notes by crossing out incorrect words and writing the correct words nearby; filling in gaps; completing incomplete thoughts; clarifying statements using his own words; adding points, definitions, colors, pictures, and references; marking important points; writing questions that remain from the lecture; and writing new questions that come up in the process. The student can do the same on the notes that were taken on the reading before the lecture.

To find answers to questions, he can email, telephone, or meet face-to-face with the instructor, another instructor in the same course, a teaching assistant, another teaching assistant, and/or another student. Benefits of emailing questions are that the student can be very specific about the questions, include many questions, and send them right away. The person on the receiving end can answer at his next convenience.

(2) Merge the Notes

The next step is to merge the lecture notes with the notes that were taken on the reading before the lecture. One way to do this is to put a line through parts of the pre-lecture notes that are the same as corresponding parts of the lecture notes. Then, take what remains, and place like information with like information.

The merged notes can be color-coded. For example, words from the pre-lecture notes can be written in blue and words from the lecture notes can be written in black. This depicts a difference in level of importance. If time runs out, the lecture notes are most important.

(3) Re-organize the Notes

Re-organize the merged notes into test format, note cards, box charts, tables, flow charts, mind maps, images, diagrams, illustrations, bullet points, hyphenated points, symbols, commas, semicolons, colons, lines, and/or arrows.

Test Format: The merged notes can be rewritten in test format. For example, if the test will be in multiple-choice format, the student can write simple multiple-choice questions and provide the answer after each question. Here, the student is thinking in the "right" format throughout the review process.

Note Cards: Merged notes can be re-organized onto note cards (index cards or flashcards). "I'm a math major," a student at the University of California at Davis said. "For every formula or concept I need to memorize, I make one small flashcard. Having the formulas on cards also makes it easier to find the formulas later." An anonymous student explained, "I write important formulas, definitions, and concepts on note cards." Some students place a question (or key word) on one side of the card, and the answer (or a matching phrase) on the other side of the card. For foreign language courses, one strategy is to draw a picture on one side of the card and the foreign word on the other side. There is an association between the picture and the foreign word without the interference of English words. Other ways of re-organizing merged notes are below.

Box Charts and Tables: Each column is assigned to a different category and each row is assigned to a different characteristic of the categories. Alternatively, each row is assigned to a different category and each column is assigned to a different characteristic of the categories. Box charts and tables are particularly useful where important details need to be classified, distinguished, or memorized. Even the smallest of charts and tables can make a difference. Some students have fun making charts; switching elements, columns and rows; and seeing what new relationships they can find. A student at Stanford University advised, "Note the basic patterns, relationships, directions, or messages (hidden or not hidden) that each chart, table, and graph depicts. Pretend that the graph is trying to tell you something; listen closely."

Flow Charts: Flow charts can provide overviews of processes, individual steps in processes, and associations between components, including cause-and-effect relationships. One student used flow charts to study the many steps of a human immune response. Another student used flow charts as road maps for the many reactions that he learned in organic chemistry.

Mind Maps: These are similar to flow charts. A key word or image is placed in the center of the page. Main ideas, represented by key words or key images, branch from this center image. Subsequent branches are represented with subsequent key words and images.

Images, Diagrams, and Illustrations: Replace words (even those inside of box charts, flow charts, and tables) with some form of simple clear image. This is effective because more than thirty percent of the brain is engineered to interpret images.

Any sentences that remain should be "crunched" and condensed into incomplete phrases, bullet points, hyphenated points, symbols, commas, semicolons, colons, lines, arrows, and lines with arrows. Lines with arrows can depict process, direction, and how individual items relate to each other.

(4) Mnemonics

The fourth step is to take the re-organized/condensed notes and apply items to them that facilitate long-term memory: Acronyms; acrostics; links; word and number associations; memory bridges; familiar groupings, objects, sequences, examples, and songs.

Acronyms: The first letter of each item, word, or phrase to be memorized is used to create a new word that may be more easily remembered. "For example, to create an acronym for the phrase, 'Volunteers in Service to America', the first letter of each of these words is placed in sequence to result in the acronym, 'VISTA.'" One strategy is to choose a word that gives clues to the items to be memorized. The acronym does not have to fit exactly. The key is for it to be memorable. One way to make the acronym memorable is to choose one that is exaggerated, personal, funny, or silly. An online source for acronyms is libraryspot.com/acronyms.htm.

Acrostics: The first letter of each item is used to create a new sentence, instead of a new word. For example, in computer science, "the seven layers of the Open Systems Interconnection model are the following: Application, Presentation, Session, Transport, Network, Data Link, and Physical. Taking the first letter from each of these words from left to right, we can create the sentence, 'All Programmers Seem To Need Daily Pizza.' From right to left, we can create the sentence, 'Please Do Not Throw Sausage Pizza Away.'" "The lines on the treble staff in music are E, G, B, D, and F. These letters can be used to create the phrase, 'Every Good Boy Deserves Favor.'" "The horizons of soil are the following: O, A1, A2, B, C, and R. These can be used to create the phrase, 'Only

Academically Active Boys Can Read.'"

Another strategy is to create a sentence or story using the key words themselves (and/or syllables within the key words) instead of the first letter in each of the key words. The more ridiculous the story, the more likely it will be remembered. The mind remembers clear images and extreme events very well.

The student can relate things to be learned to personal experiences; significant or popular events, people, places, or dates; or things that are otherwise familiar or meaningful.

Word and Number Associations: As one student at Central Michigan University told, "When my young son kept misspelling 'decide' and 'beside' in a spelling lesson, I told him that when he thinks of 'decide,' let his mind see D.C., as in Washington D.C., where decisions are made. When he thinks of 'beside,' let his mind see B.S. He, being young, thought that thinking B.S. was amusing."

A student at the University of Michigan at Dearborn said that a few years ago, he was trying to remember his license plate number, LPE 622. At the time, he was working in a job that he absolutely hated. He realized that the "LPE" part of his license plate number could represent "Long Painful Eternity", which was how he felt about his job. The "622" part of his license plate number reminded him of the last three digits of his telephone number. The first number was one less and the last two numbers were one more. He didn't have that license plate number anymore but said that he will always remember it.

Familiar Groupings: "One technique which has been useful to me, especially in remembering certain numbers," a student at the Massachusetts Institute of Technology explained, "has been to group the unfamiliar number into patterns the brain is already familiar with, i.e., groups of three and four (as in a phone number) or groups of five (like zip codes). A while back I was challenging myself to memorize a couple hundred digits of the decimal expansion of pi as a mental exercise, just to see how good my memory was. Strangely enough, once I memorized the first 100 or so digits, and began mentally repeating them to myself, I found that my brain preferred to remember the numbers in tiny groups, instead of individually. For example, I remember the first 100 digits of pi as:

3.14 159 26535 8979 323 846 264 338 327 950 288 419 716 93993 7510 5820 9749 4459 230 78164 06286 20899 86280 34825 34211 70679

The first thing that struck me about these number groupings of three, four, and five is that they are number lengths that humans are used to dealing with on a daily basis. Once I realized that my brain preferred to remember things in this manner, I pre-divided the next 100 digits of pi into similar groups that stood out to me, many of them ending up like imaginary phone numbers in groups of three and four. I was able to memorize the next 100 digits in less than an hour doing it this way. Something about seeing those familiar number lengths really helps."

Bridges: "I build 'memory bridges,'" a student at Brigham Young University remarked. "What I mean by that is that I focus on one fact, which reminds me of another, and so on. This way I don't have to worry about remembering everything because certain facts cue the other information."

Objects: A student at the University of Florida studies in the room where the examination will take place and associates what she is learning to individual objects in the examination room. During the examination, the objects in the room remind her of what she learned.

Common Sequence: "A memory technique that I have found consistently useful," a student at Oxford University said, "is to memorize facts, figures, diagrams, or concepts against a common journey or sequence. More specifically, I have used the suits in a pack of cards as a useful template. In short, for each aspect of a problem, I assign a new card. For example, to remember British government majorities, I use a different card for each majority. This technique is useful if you need to remember sequences. While not immediately intuitive, it is surprising how well it effectively 'locks in' the knowledge." There are other examples of attaching information to be learned to a common journey. One is to mentally attach information to each of the buildings or other permanent objects that one sees on the way to class. Another example is to mentally attach an item to each of the components of a stick figure. One item is mentally attached to the feet, one to the legs, one to the torso, one to the neck, and one to the head.

Examples: "For abstract concepts, attach a specific example to the concept that is being learned," a student at the University of California at Los Angeles suggested. "In the future, the specific example will immediately remind you of the true meaning of the concept."

Songs: A student at the University of Michigan at Dearborn claimed, "If you put what you are learning into a song, you are almost certain to remember it. Hey, I bet you can still recall a few episodes of 'School House Rock.'" "I had a friend in German class who claimed that every poem can be set to the theme music from 'Gilligan's Island,'" a student at Georgia Institute of Technology recalled, "and I have yet to prove her wrong!" The student can use words that rhyme. One student at the University of Illinois made a rap song from the steps of the citric acid cycle in biology.

Overlap: The student can use more than one mnemonic device for items that are particularly important or difficult to recall.

Confidence: As a student at Virginia Polytechnic Institute and State University said, "When you have to remember something, consciously choose to remember. Believe yourself into strong confidence: you have good ability to remember those things."

SECTION 8B: OFFICE HOURS

8B.1 General Points

General comments about office hours included the following eight responses: "My favorite professor told us: 'Office hours are the best-kept secret of academic life.' Probably that's why nobody realizes how valuable they really are"; "I find professors more than willing to help students in office hours, in part because they are so under utilized in this capacity"; "Don't be bothered if you are the only one who shows up to an office hour. You should expect this...It's lonely at the top"; "Office hours are opportunities to ask questions that could not be asked in class or other settings"; "Asking questions until you completely understand is part of taking responsibility for your education. It increases the accuracy of your understanding"; "Never forget that if you are paying tuition, you are paying in part for your professors' and teaching assistants' time"; "A common mistake is to think that you can obtain an A+ by yourself. It is usually not possible to get an A+ without constantly bothering the teacher or teaching assistant for help with homeworks or working in groups"; "Sometimes the difference between who will do better in the class has to do with which students make the effort to understand the material with the professors help."

8B.2 When to Attend Office Hours

"Never spend more than two hours banging your head on a problem before seeking help," a student at North Carolina State University at Raleigh insisted. "The earlier you seek an answer, the more willing they are to part with it, effectively penalizing last minute behavior." "Remember," an anonymous student said, "that there are many ways to get in contact: email, telephone, fax, and in person in office hours. If your teacher or assigned teaching assistant is not available, give your questions to the nearest teaching assistant." Some students visit professors regularly, no matter what the grade, if not with a question, just to talk. Different frequencies were presented. The lowest was three times a term. Many students suggested once a week. Some people go to every office hour session.

8B.3 Specificity

A common suggestion was to ask specific questions to increase the chance of getting an answer that meets the student's specific needs. Some people go further and explain why they are asking the question or why they are having trouble with these particular points. This helps to clarify matters.

As mentioned earlier, some students place marks or post-it notes at the site of a problem in their notes or in the book, and bring these to office hours. With this, the teacher learns the context of the question.

A student at the University of California at Berkeley begins by telling the teacher that she has been attending the classes, completing all of the readings, and that these questions came up during the process. This is to let the teacher know that she is not asking because she has been goofing off but that these questions came up despite having done the expected work. It also allows the teacher to focus in on the question at hand without feeling that he needs to re-explain something that has already been explained in class.

It is useful to give the instructor feedback on the level of specificity as well. Let the instructor know specifically what you heard and how you heard it. Detail your interpretation of what you heard from him for him.

8B.4 Probing

Office hours are additional opportunities to continue the process of probing for areas of importance. As a student at the University of Kentucky at Lexington remarked, "Each professor has his or her own 'secret agenda'—the most important issue, model, concern, etc. that she wants every student to remember for life." Some instructors are good at clarifying areas of importance on their own. Others need it coaxed out of them.

8B.5 Quality

Every once in a while, ask the teacher, "Are you happy with the quality of my work? Are you happy with my progress? Is there anything that I can do to improve the quality?" Sometimes the assessor is happy with most of the work but dissatisfied with one or two elements. It is best to find out what these are before it is too late. The student needs to probe for the assessor's perception of the quality to date, particularly in classes where there are highly subjective components in the system of evaluation. Some students only find out what was going on in the teacher's or advisor's mind when the student reads the evaluation in shock.

8B.6 The Cutting Edge

A student at Carnegie Mellon University asks questions not only about the class material but also about the professor's research and other cutting-edge research in the field. Sometimes she reads about each before arriving. She tries to give the professor questions that he might not have considered in his own research. She said that A+ students can almost become sounding boards for the teacher's theories. Both parties can benefit. The student learns more than what is in class and in the book. The teacher receives a perspective that is not biased by the traditions of the field.

8B.7 Stay In the Right Direction

"On all projects ask the instructor if you are thinking and headed in the right direction," a student at the University of Greenwich in England suggested. "Ask for advice; try to apply this advice and improve your technique at each step."

8B.8 That Extra Something

"Remember," a student at Yale University said, "the difference between first place and second place is often one small piece of information. This is sometimes acquired in office hours by communicating with the person who knows the most about the subject, the professor. It can happen inadvertently; it can fall into the student's lap without the student nor the professor knowing it."

8B.9 Corrections

In office hours, the student can inform the instructor about problematic patterns in the class. "In one of my calculus classes," an anonymous student explained, "the professor discussed 'wedge spaces' with the class for the last two weeks of the term. He was writing a book, which was to cover this topic but wedge spaces was not in our book. I was doing well in the class and did not understand this topic. In the last week, I went to his office hours. I pointed out that I had the highest grade in the class thus far but did not understand the topic, and that other students did not understand it either. I added that his forthcoming book should be helpful to future classes. He left the topic completely out of the final." Something that is a problem for one student can also be a problem for other people but someone needs to speak up and tell the instructor. Teachers are on a different level, have different lives, and may not be aware of all of the missing links at the student level even though the teachers are the ones teaching the class. Other times an instructor is aware of a problem but not of its extent. Relating differences to the instructor can be helpful for other reasons too. "If you think the professor's guidelines do not fit your needs as a student, negotiate for a change that does (but meets the same standard)," a student at Columbia University said. "Sometimes the professor will agree that a change is needed."

Problems in scoring can also be resolved in office hours. "Keep a close watch on scoring," a student at Brigham Young University advised. "Professors have a lot of students and mistakes are made. At least one time per semester, one of my grades is wrong." "Based on my experience," a student at Pennsylvania State University said, "about 20-30% of all errors that were found in my homeworks by graders were THEIR mistakes, not mine." Sometimes, some instructors scan some parts without looking closely. A student at Brigham Young University suggested that "If there are some questionable marks, bring them to the teacher's attention. Part of being an A+ student is being assertive enough to know what you deserve." In some cases, there is a misinterpretation of what was meant in writing and some extra explanation is all that is needed. "One thing that most students neglect to do is bargain with the professor about the grade they get for their assignments and homeworks," a student at Pennsylvania State University said. "Some students believe that this kind of bargaining can result in a negative attitude of the instructor. In my opinion, this is completely wrong. If you can make your case, this will show your confidence, and knowledge of the subject.

Even if you made a mistake that is not trivial, your desire to understand the roots of it will be met with respect. However, this might not work with some particularly arrogant people who are not willing to hear that they are wrong."

The student can also correct her own understanding. A student at Indiana University of Pennsylvania asked questions about items that she was not really sure about on assignments and tests that have been returned even if she got the answers right and received a high score. This increased the standard of her understanding, prepared her for future challenges, and showed the instructor that she was interested in understanding.

8B.10 Demonstrate

Beyond class, assignments, and tests, office hours are further opportunities for the student to demonstrate what he knows and to stand out from other students. Among other things, the student can show his commitment to the learning process, interest in what is being taught, desire to understand the roots of the issues, earnest effort to take advantage of all that the class has to offer, extra work that he has done to find answers to relevant questions, intellectual curiosity, enthusiasm, and character. The instructor absorbs this information at conscious and subconscious levels.

8B.11 Objective and Subjective

"Learn to understand that the professor and the student both have specific goals, are both human, and that a grade is very much a negotiation that has both objective and subjective parts," a student at

Georgia Institute of Technology said. "Many highly intelligent people concentrate heavily on the objective portion but do not pay enough attention to the personal aspects of the student-teacher relationship mainly because conventional wisdom condemns 'kissing up.' Cultivating a constructive relationship that demonstrates to the professor that you are interested in learning, and have a respect for the limitations that the classroom environment places on the professor and student is in my opinion AT LEAST 30% of your grade. Even 'heartless' professors will subconsciously help a student when the professor feels that the student is contributing an equal part to the process."

"Whether teachers admit it or not," a student at the University of Pennsylvania insisted, "there is always an area at the boundary between an A and an A+ that comes down to whether the person handing out your final grade has had positive contact with you."

8B.12 Benefit of the Doubt

An anonymous student suggested that "Regular participation in office hours also establishes some reserve. If something unexpected happens or if you are on the borderline, the teacher will give you the benefit of the doubt." Another student, at Indiana University of Pennsylvania, stated, "A professor won't let you fail if you are consulting with him on a regular basis." A student at Louisiana State University said that if a committee meets that is reviewing your progress, the professor will argue in your favor. "Getting to know your professors also helps out a lot when it comes time to apply for scholarships, graduate schools, or a job" a student at the University of South Dakota offered. "People look very highly of college professors' recommendations."

8B.13 One on One

Some of the students explained that it is easier to retain information received directly from the teacher on a "one on one" basis. Some explained that maintaining a positive relationship with the teacher is enriching and makes learning fun.

SECTION 8C: ABOUT ASSIGNMENTS

8C.1 When to Start

Some instructors do not provide information about assignments in advance. Instead, an instructor might tell the students in the class about the assignment when the instructor is ready to do so. In such cases, some students suggested starting the assignment on the same day that the homework is assigned, even if it is not due for some time. This gets things started while the information is still in mind; generates momentum; and creates both a sense of progress and progress itself.

8C.2 Give Yourself Instructions

A student at Columbia University said, "Give yourself instructions. Determine what you will do and the limitations of what you will do before starting anything. This will keep you directed."

8C.3 Target the Right Question

Read the question very carefully and address that specific question. Common mistakes are to address a slightly different question, to do some parts of a question but not others, and to focus on extra parts instead of or before the actual requirements.

8C.4 Know the Intent of the Assignment

Take a moment to ask why an assignment was given. As a student at Clemson University explained, "It has been my experience that if I will take a few minutes to try and figure out why the assignment was given to me (or in the case of a test, to find the concepts that are being covered) before I become too involved in the details of the task at hand, the completion of the project becomes much easier, and my performance is usually improved over just jumping right in and working."

8C.5 Review a Previous Publication

For almost any assignment, there is some form of previous publication on the topic. This is true for both small and large assignments. Students offered the following advice: "Read and critique articles that both use the techniques you are learning and relate to your primary interest in the field"; "If you are required to critique someone else's published work, get some information about the writer, criticisms about the writer, or analysis of the writer's work. You can learn the author's biases, strengths, and weaknesses"; "There is always a previous standard of some sort. Read about it so that you don't reinvent the wheel and so that you can make some educated decisions about what to do next."

8C.6 Cite Sources

"Cite sources even when it's not needed to give the work more credibility." Add a reference section or bibliography even when these are not required. One benefit of a bibliography is that it can include sources cited in the paper, as well as additional sources for further reading.

8C.7 Don't Limit Yourself

"Don't limit yourself to definite 'answers' or 'solutions.'" Consider the circumstances in which an answer is true and in which it is false. At what point does it stop being true and why? What are the assumptions? What are the challenges, complexities, and dynamics? Does the mathematical answer match physical intuition? One extra sentence about one or more of these can result in a more accurate and thorough answer.

8C.8 Relate the Topic of Study to Everyday Life or Industry

Some students ask the teacher directly about industrial applications of the topic at hand; the students then expand from this point of information. Some look for journal reviews on the everyday or industrial applications of the topic. Others yet contact people who are considered to be "gurus" in the field. They ask the gurus about current practices at the cutting edge of the field, and future directions of the topic.

Some students already know who the gurus in their field are. Others find out who the gurus in their field are by consulting performance indicators, like "Essential Science Indicators," produced by the Institute for Scientific Information; citation, periodical, bibliographical, or book review indexes; and/or a "who's who" directory of the field. Some go to web sites that index experts like allexperts.com, expertcentral.com, experts.yahoo.com, and libraryspot.com/askanexpert.htm. Many of these experts are willing to answer questions for free. Some university library web sites include clickable links to experts in or associated with the university who are willing to answer questions emailed from the school's students. Some students find experts in their field by going to the web site of their particular department, of departments on the subject at other universities, of trade organizations of the subject, or of discussion groups on the topic.

8C.9 Search the Internet

"Learn how to search the Internet and you can become an expert on a topic of choice," a student at Stanford University said. "Go to a web site that has a search tool, type in a word or phrase to be searched, and click on the search or submit button. The search tool will return results which contain (or in some way match) the chosen words."

There are seven basic categories of search tools on the Internet: subject directories; search engines; directories with search engines; meta-search engines; specialty database engines; news readers for subject-based discussion groups; and readers for chat rooms.

Subject directories are easy-to-browse directories of subjects, organized (by people, not computers) in a hierarchical structure from basic to more specific categories. Since subject directories only cover a small fraction of the pages available on the Internet, they are most effective for finding general and well-organized information on a topic. Some subject directories return results with links to more specific references. Traditionally popular web sites with subject directories include Yahoo and Look Smart. Some subject directories that have traditionally been useful for academics include Argus Clearinghouse, About, Librarians' Index to the Internet, Internet Public Library, and the World Wide Web Virtual Library.

Search engines are a second way to search the Internet. Search engines rely on computer programs called spiders or robots to crawl the web and scan for the search words. They often return thousands of results. They are not as organized as subject directories. However, search engines can be effective for finding very specific and up-to-date information. Popular web sites that have search engines include Google, Lycos, Altavista, Hotbot, Excite, Northern Light, One Key, Go, and Snap. The Spider's Apprentice, at Monash.com, rates major search engines. A list of over

260 search engines in more than 18 categories is located at refdesk.com/newsrch.html

Directories with search engines are a third way to search the Internet. These have both subject directories and search engines. Many sites that have traditionally had either a subject directory or a search engine are now creating hybrids of the two features or other features. Examples of sites with hybrids include Yahoo, Google, Altavista, Hotbot, Excite, Northern Light, Web Crawler, One Key, Go, and Snap.

Meta-search engines are a fourth way to search the Internet. They search several search engines at once. Examples of sites with meta-search engines are Search, Ixquick, Excite, Dogpile, C4, MetaCrawler, ProFusion, Mamma, SavvySearch, Cyber411, WebTaxi, Debriefing, SherlockHound, InfoZoid, and FindSpot.

Specialty database engines represent a fifth tool for searching the Internet. They are designed to collect relevant sites for particular subject areas. An example is Achoo!, which collects medical and health sites. FindLaw collects legal sites. Web sites with indexes of specialty databases include Search, Beaucoup, Complete Planet, Price's Direct Search, Internets, and Invisible Web. "Invisible Web" is a term which describes parts of the World Wide Web which are difficult to search. An additional list of tools to search "invisible" parts of the web is located at libraryspot.com/features/invisibleweb.htm.

Of course, the World Wide Web is a popular part of the Internet but there are other parts of the Internet too. Many colleges, research groups, non-profit organizations, businesses, and government agencies have useful information stored on their computer systems that can be searched through means other than the World Wide Web. For example, FTP (File Transfer Protocol) sites are known to be good sites to download, and sometimes upload documents, music, or video. Oth.net and software programs like Archie can search for FTP sites. Gopher sites are sites that often contain a variety of useful resource types and links. Veronica is a software program that can search for Gopher sites. WAIS (Wide Area Information Server) clients can effectively search databases of remote computers. Telnet is also a common way to connect to some remote computers. Hytelnet is a software program that can search for telnet sites by keyword.

Subject-based discussion groups represent a sixth search tool. Subject-based discussion groups are sometimes referred to as newsgroups, forums, or conferences. There are tens of thousands of these discussion groups online. They range from basic to highly specialized topics of discussion. Usenet is the most common platform for discussion groups; it divides groups into major categories called "hierarchies." A master list of hierarchies is posted at magma.ca/~leisen/mlnh/. The main categories of Usenet discussion groups are Computer Science, Science, Humanities, Business, Social, Recreation, Alternative, Miscellaneous, News (which covers Usenet, the Internet, and software), and Talk (which includes current events, politics, and religion).

These main categories of Usenet are divided into a large number of subcategories, which define individual discussion groups. To search, browse, read, and post messages to a discussion group, a type of software called a "news reader" is needed. For PC, news readers include News Xpress, Noworyta, Gravity, Agent, and WinVN. For Macintosh, news readers include News Hopper, Inter News, and News Watcher. A software program called Nographer can translate Usenet into a web site in a browser. Some of these software programs can be downloaded at download.com or zdnet.com. Conveniently, some popular browsers like Netscape and Internet Explorer have built-in news readers. Instructions on the use of these built-in news readers are available in the "help" section of the browser. The web site Google (through its "Groups" section) has options to search, read, and post to newsgroups directly through its web site. Subject-based e-mail or discussion lists are options too. A good web site for this is lsoft.com/lists/listref.html. A directory of scholarly and professional e-conferences is available at kovacs.com/directory/.

One difference between discussion groups and chat rooms is that communication in chat rooms is done in real time. IRC (Internet Relay Chat) is the original and most popular medium for chat. Software clients for IRC include mIRC for PC and Ircle for Macintosh. A second medium for Internet chat is IMC (Instant Message Chat), which requires what is referred to as "messenger" software (e.g. of ICQ, AOL, Yahoo, or MSN). A third medium for Internet chat is "web page chat." Web page chat requires a java-capable web browser. A MUD (Multiple User Dimension, Multiple User Dialogue or Multiple User Dungeon) is a computer program which people can log into. Each person controls a computerized character. One of the options is chat. Client software for MUD can be acquired from ftp.tcp.com. A large list of MUDs is available at mudlist.eorbit.net.

Many students pick and consistently use one or two of their favorite Internet search tools. Once she has chosen a search tool, the student is advised to learn the search tool's rules for use of keywords, synonyms, quotation marks, and Boolean operators like "and," "or," and "not." This is to increase the chance of isolating what the student is looking for in a search. Search tool rules are usually described in the "help" section or the FAQ (Frequently Asked Questions) section of the search tool, web site, or database. To find a web site that explains an issue or item, the person can in some cases include FAQ as one of the keywords in the search box. In this case, some search tools will return a list of web pages that explain the basics of the chosen topic.

Once the student has found a web site with information, he must be careful about the legitimacy of the information that is on the web site. Many individual school departments or their individual libraries have web sites which list reference sites that are useful for their particular subject area and authoritative in nature. One online source for libraries is libraryspot.com/libraries/. Many major trade groups, societies, and associations for subject areas have web sites with authoritative references too. The Mayfield Quick View Guides include Internet resources for specific subject areas. Some students use their favorite Internet browser to bookmark web sites that they feel may be useful for future use.

8C.10 Look at Your Work Through the Teacher's Eyes

Scrutinize assignments from the teacher's perspective. How would the teacher respond to each element? What assessment of quality would he or she make for each of these elements and steps? What things would he or she find refreshing, new, exciting, or just average? What things would he or she want to see? What questions would he or she have?

8C.11 Be Creative

Responses from students included the following: "Logical as well as creative skills are key"; "Respect conventional thinking whilst coming up with your own opinions all of the time." "Aim at exciting a bored examiner"; "Try to surprise the instructor"; "Tell Dr. X something that he or she does not already know"; "Evidence of thought and synthesis will get you an A+, and you'll be less bored for it"; "Work until you think you've earned an A+; then make at least three improvements"; "One additional insight, one unique way of synthesizing an idea, or one shred of original thought expressed clearly puts you ahead"; "Even something small that is slightly original is often enough to distinguish you from the person in second place."

8C.12 Think Across Lines

Responses from students included the following: "Apply lateral thinking"; "From a holistic viewpoint, there is no one system that cannot be correlated to any other. Once you identify (or create) a basic skeleton that a subject can be reduced to, look at how the new subject can also hang from that same framework"; "Relate it to a smaller or a larger structure"; "Always look for new ways to make connections. New links can sometimes be found by using new resources"; "Consider a textbook or authority that disagrees and attempt to reconcile the two points of view."

8C.13 Hard Part Verses Easy Part

Some people do the hard or boring part of an assignment first. The idea is that they have the most energy and time at the beginning of the process. The hard part gets done completely before energy and time wear down. Some students also apply this to deciding the order of hard verses easy assignments. "As the night drags on," a student at the University of California at Berkeley claimed, "the less likely it becomes that you will even do the hard assignment that you have been dreading, let alone do it well. So do the hard assignment first and the easy assignment second; then both will get done."

Some students in the survey pool do the opposite. They do the easy assignment first and the hard assignment second. The argument is that the quick success of an easy assignment builds confidence and momentum towards the hard assignment.

8C.14 Storage

It is wise to keep copies of each stage of work. In some cases, the student will want to revert back to an earlier version of the work. She may find that a piece that was thrown out is now valuable. Other human errors can take place. In one of my classes, a teacher lost my paper. She did not apologize for losing it and even blamed me for not having a back-up copy of the document; unfortunately, when things go wrong, people choose interpretations that keep themselves protected. The student can keep himself protected by storing each stage of work. Some people store each step on computer disks. A student at Indiana University of Pennsylvania stores copies on his computer hard drive but also on two floppy disks to have electronic back-ups of the work. Printing hard copies of each stage of work can offer a high level of protection. This can protect against the effects of computer viruses and mechanical failures.

8C.15 Take Every Assignment Seriously

Responses from students included the following: "I saw that my grades improved rapidly when I forgot about the final grade and made sure that every single paper, project, and test I worked on was done to the best of my ability. The catch is to apply this to every individual assignment no matter how big or small"; "Approach each assignment with the same level of preparation and effort. No assignment is trivial"; "For every assignment, ask yourself this: Am I proud of this work? Does it demonstrate my full potential as a student?"; "Don't compare yourself to others; always endeavor to achieve something more or better than your previous achievements. If the assignment asks for one thing, broaden that to include associated issues or items; enrich yourself more than you might have with the stated assignment. Seize opportunities for enrichment"; "Consistently outdo yourself, and reach new standards of excellence"; "Be serious about assignments that have to be turned in but also about assignments that do not have to be turned in. These assignments can let you know whether or not you are understanding the material"; "If the work does not have to be turned in, turn it in anyway;

this sends a strong message to the instructor."

8C.16 Take Every Class Seriously

Responses from participants included the following: "You tell yourself, 'Every course is EQUAL.' That means 'Sociology' = 'Zoology.' While one requires a great deal more study and effort, the other requires a good bit of diligence to produce the 'A+.' Tell yourself 'IT COUNTS' and do the work during pleasant activity."; "Don't assume that one's aptitude for the material is higher than the majority of the others in the class"; "Even if you have a string of victories, take every single class seriously!"; "Don't expect it all to come easily to you. Even if you are really smart and on top of things, there can always be that class that may be an unexpected disaster. Mine was Nature Study."

8C.17 Learn It Now

Learn it now because you'll need it later. Information often builds on itself within and between courses. For example, the information in Calculus 1 will be needed to understand Calculus 2, Calculus 3, and future mathematics courses.

8C.18 Understand It

Responses included the following: "Understand as much as possible to reduce how much you have to memorize. For example, if you understand what is behind a formula, you can figure yourself out of a mess"; "The top students will not only be able to apply equations but they will also understand where these equations come from and what their limitations are"; "The trick is to understand how a formula or process is derived or how it is trying to accomplish its task. Then you don't have to remember the specifics and you will be considerably more likely to re-deduct a greater number of concepts than recall facts. A very simple example is addition: If you can remember how to count and follow a number line, you can always add any two numbers by counting along that number line without even having to do 'long addition.' You will never be dead in the water if you can't recall what 7+8 is."

8C.19 Question Yourself

If you are having trouble with something, ask yourself why is it that you are having trouble? What characteristics of the parts of this issue are a problem for you? What parts of it are not a problem? Which components are true and which are not true? Why are they true or not true? The right questions can get the student moving in the right direction and sometimes all of the way to the answer.

8C.20 Trial and Error

"Take full advantage of laboratory sessions," a student at the University of Illinois at Chicago said. "Also, try practical examples like building the circuit described in the book. See what it does in reality to better understand the problem. Some of the steps require trial and error. These steps can be frustrating but you will learn from them, and be able to apply what you learned from them to future challenges."

A student at Indiana University obtained her own copy of the computer software for a class. She played around with it BEFORE the class and identified peculiarities and bugs that always exist in a system. Such bugs are often not explained in class nor in the manual. When something didn't work, she made a slight change and tried again from a different angle. Trial and error is a useful strategy for assigned homework too. If a student has difficulty, she can try from other angles to get to the next step. Trial and error is part of academics and life. In fact, research conducted by faculty and "Research and Development" conducted by businesses are forms of trial and error. One professor in a famous laboratory said that only one out of ten of the ideas in his laboratory work but when he finds the one that works, it is well worth the effort of the ten tries.

8C.21 Pros and Cons

A student at Stanford University said, "Everything in life has pros and cons. Take the time to list and then weigh the pros and cons of each option. This can be an effective way to eliminate options that are less likely and recognize those that are more likely. It can also strengthen your final argument. If this information is included in your written assignment, it shows the instructor that you are thinking objectively about the options."

8C.22 Use the Units of Measurement

Often an answer can be found by studying the units of measurements. The units of measurement of variables given in a word problem can often be used to navigate towards the units of measurement of the variable to be solved. For example, if the variable to be solved is molar energy and the expected units of measurement are joules per mole, the units of measurement of the variables that are given in the word problem can be algebraically converted so that units (or a combination of components of units) that equal joules are directed to the numerator and units (or a combination of components of units) that equal moles are directed to the denominator. This "brute force" method is often effective because at the end of the day, all units have to match up. Considering units of measurement is also a quick way to double-check final answers that are expected to be in a particular range or specific units.

8C.23 Chaos to Categories

One way to deal with chaos is to force it into categories. Divide each category into smaller categories and each of the smaller categories into smaller categories. This creates an organized grid from which to answer a question. It can also work in the opposite direction. Find the closest subcategory or create one. Build up to larger categories. This creates a grid from which to operate.

Chaos can be placed into other types of categories too. Examples include: important and unimportant; true verses untrue; and likely verses unlikely. Levels can be used for categories. Examples include various levels of importance and various levels of likelihood.

Confusion can be placed into an outline. Further outlines can be made at higher or lower levels for remaining trouble spots. Disorder can be forced into the basic categories, who, what, where, when, how, or why. Once information is placed into categories, it is no longer chaos.

8C.24 Context

Another way to deal with difficult information is to change the context. Go to a lower or higher level. Try a more basic or more specific level. Stand back from it all or stand closer to it all, and look at it again.

Change the location or order of the pieces. Add or remove pieces of it.

8C.25 Write Down What You Will Do Next

"I find that it helps to just write down the number of the next problem I have to do," a student at the University of Wisconsin-Eau Claire explained. "If I take a break or if I'm getting tired, I will come back to that problem and do it." A similar approach is for the student to write down what he hopes to accomplish in his next session. The process of coming back will be easier because the strategy and goals for the session will already be defined.

8C.26 Develop a Step-by-Step Method

For word problems, it is useful to develop a step-by-step method. One method that is effective for some science word problems follows. Step one: read the passage. Step two: write the symbol of the variable that is to be solved followed by a question mark. For example, if "acceleration" is the variable to be solved, and "a" is its symbol, the student can write "a?" Step three: write the symbols and values of variables that are given in the passage. For example, the passage might provide the information that force, whose symbol is "F," is 15 newtons; the symbol for newtons is "N." The passage might also state that mass, whose symbol is "m," is 5 kilograms; the symbol for kilograms is "kg." So, for this step, the student can write the information in short form: F = 15 N and m = 5 kg. Step four: think of an equation that includes the given variables and the variable to be solved. For example, the student might have learned in class or from a textbook, an equation that includes all of the variables, like force equals mass times acceleration (F = ma). Step five: when needed, algebraically convert the equation to equal the variable to be solved. In our example, the variable to be solved is acceleration; the equation learned in class, force equals mass times acceleration (F = ma), can be algebraically converted to the equation, acceleration equals force divided by mass (a = F/m). Step six: fill in the equation with the given values and compute (a = 15 N/5 kg = 15 meter kg /5 kg s^2 = 3 meters/s^2 = 3 meters per seconds squared). This is the answer for our hypothetical example. The seven-step method just described is one approach. Some students develop a step-by-step method for each main type of word problem in the class.

8C.27 Practice Makes Perfect

"In classes where problem-solving is important," an anonymous student advised, "practice applying equations over and over to gain fluency in the mechanics. You will also discover subtleties that tend to show up on examinations."

"If you want to be good at anything," a student at Clemson University said, "you have to practice. I don't care whether you are kicking field goals, shooting a firearm, or taking tests. If you practice something enough, when you get to the test, it will just be another set of problems to work."

A student at Stanford University insisted, "Now is the time to make mistakes. In fact, the purpose of practice is to find your mistakes now so that you are not making as many of them at test time."

A student at the University of Illinois made the following comparison. "As in a military operation, planning, practicing, and training requires about 20 to 100 hours compared to the actual event.... Think about it: military pilots fly about 500 hours per year just for training missions plus much more time in ground school and in mission briefings and debriefings.

Combat missions last about 2.5 hours (or less); less than 2 minutes are actually engaged with the enemy. The same is true for academics. To be prepared to do well on a 3-hour examination, you have to have put in your flight hours well before the event."

8C.28 Practice Questions

"First, do problems for which there are answers in the textbook," a student at the University of Oregon suggested. "This gives you a good start and lets you know if you are doing the problems correctly."

"I pick the five hardest questions in the back of the chapter that are not assigned," a student at Columbia University said. "I do as much as I can on these; then, I go over the parts of the five questions that I could not figure out with the professor or with one of the teaching assistants BEFORE I start the assigned homework questions for the chapter. The knowledge that I gain from the answers of the five hardest questions allows me to do well on the assigned homework problems. It also means that I will get those one or two really hard questions on the test that everyone else misses."

"A proven strategy for me," a student at Stanford University remarked, "has been to do all of the odd numbered questions at the end of a chapter the weekend before a test. Test questions are of comparable difficulty to these questions and sometimes are nothing more than modifications of them. I can check the answers in the back of the book to make sure I understand what I am doing. If I have less time, I begin with the questions on concepts that I do not clearly understand so that I do not have any gaping weaknesses come test time." "Before the examination," a student at the University of California at Davis remarked, "I do 'random problem time' because I am in a scientific field and most test questions are problem solving. I go to the homework problems in the book that were not assigned and attempt to do them." An anonymous student said, "I do problems that are related to concepts that are in bold, color, or italics; these are likely the most important concepts." One person at the University of Pennsylvania determines which type of questions show up most often on homework assignments and old examinations; he focuses 75% of his time on doing these types of questions. "For CSC courses, I found doing practice exams most helpful. The professor might give out a packet or one can find a packet from others. Sometimes, you can find tests online. I find that I usually need 5 practice exams per exam to guarentee a spot in the 90's," a student at North Carolina State University at Raleigh said. "Otherwise, potluck."

Creating Your Own Examination: Some students rewrite their lecture notes in the form of an examination. Some create examination questions on separate paper instead. "Create your self-test in the format that the examination will be in," a student at Indiana University of Pennsylvania suggested. "If it is multiple-choice, go back to your notes and think of multiple-choice questions they could ask (and what they will try to confuse you with). If it is fill-in the blank format, write sentences with blanks. If it is essay format, think of main themes; prepare main point outlines for anticipated questions. The outlines might include a couple of specific details and examples. You can even write the essay out; 99% of the time, you will get some of the essays from the ones you thought up. Don't expect to be able to anticipate all of the questions. Getting a few of them (or similar ones) makes the process of thinking of them in advance worthwhile." "I like to think of the most difficult questions," a student at Yale University said. "If I can't answer them, I take them to office hours and have a teaching assistant or professor answer them. Then, I am prepared for the worst." A student at Hampton University mentioned, "I take self-tests under full test conditions in the test room itself."

8C.29 Working in a Group

Some students do problem sets with a group of students. Comments from some of these students included the following seven responses: "Working in a group helps me to recognize my strengths and weaknesses"; "I learn by challenging other students and having them challenge me"; "It sinks in best for me when I hear it from another student"; "No matter how difficult the question, some member of the group will know how to solve it or know how to solve it a second or third way"; "Don't leave the student group without learning 'how' and 'why' each answer is reached"; "Working in a group is good practice because in the real world professionals work together on projects. Loners are often left behind (both in the classroom and in the real world)." Some students cautioned not to depend too much on other students because there are certain paths that "you" must walk to learn what you need to learn.

8C.30 Show Your Work

A student at the University of California at Davis said that the more the graders can see of what your brain is doing, the more partial credit you can accumulate. If nine out of ten of your steps are right, and you have written these nine steps down on the paper, you might receive most of the points even if you didn't get the final answer right. Make sure to distinguish the final answer from the other steps in the process. This can be done by underlining, circling, or enclosing the final answer in a box. The distinction reduces confusion and makes things convenient for the grader. This is something that graders appreciate.

In some cases, it can be useful to explain your reasons and/or assumptions, in addition to showing your steps. Your answers may be true with your particular set of assumptions but the teacher may need to know what your assumptions are. YOU must be the one to take the initiative to list your assumptions. Otherwise, you could lose by default.

8C.31 Repetition

"Repetition is the law of learning," a student at Ricks College insisted. Students described many different systems of repetition.

Repetition with Shrinkage: Many students review their notes a few times during the course of a term, each time rewriting the notes to a more condensed form. A student at the University of California at Berkeley said, "If I take notes from my notes, and then notes from those notes at least three times during the semester, I gradually shrink the load of information so that I am down to a size that is manageable to read right before the test." "I typically reduce my notes down to twelve to fourteen sides of paper," a student at the University of Greenwich in England asserted. "In the long run, it is easier to have a condensed set of notes than endless folders and books to work from." Some students make further distinctions, for example, indicating which parts they have learned well and which parts they have not yet learned well. Some students shrink the notes down to one prioritized study sheet or add such a sheet to their shortened notes.

Audio Tape: Some students record their shortened notes onto an audiotape or CD. Then they listen to the audio version several times. The audio version can be played at times and places where it is traditionally difficult to review written notes. If the device has speed control, the process can take place quickly.

A Four-times Approach: A student at Columbia University asserted, "I use Gordon Green's approach. I correct or rewrite notes in the afternoon after each class. This is my first review. In the week before the test, I review the notes three more times: First, I breeze through the notes, not worrying about details. The second time, a couple days later, I spend more time on details. The third and final time is the day before the test."

Another Four-times Approach: A student at the University of Tulsa explained that when he is trying to learn new words, he tries to re-memorize the word in three, seven, thirty, and ninety days.

A Seven-times Approach: A student at the University of Maine "read somewhere that once you do something seven times, it becomes a habit or that you have to see something seven times before it becomes a solid memory. Whatever the case, I try to go over it as close to seven times as possible. I try to have the seven times in different formats. For example:

1) Read the material.
2) Listen to the lecture.
3) Write down everything I can.
4) Reread the material.
5) Make flash cards.
6) Read notes.
7) Talk to classmates. I ask them for help or if they need help. If I can explain the material to someone else, then I know it for sure. Even if I think I know it, I go ahead and make them think I don't. I get them to explain it to me. Maybe they have a different perspective on the material. This helps both of us."

Previous Two Lessons: "After finishing the study of a lesson," a student at the University of Florida said, "I briefly read the last two lessons just to refresh my memory."

Previous Week: A student at the University of California at Davis, spends fifteen minutes during the weekend reviewing each lecture of the last week. At student at Columbia University stated that each week he gives himself short quick quizzes. He said that this is more exciting and effective than long quizzes at infrequent intervals.

Same Day: One student at North Carolina State argued that the "time away" between exposures is what helps. He reads the information, comes back to it later, reads it again, and then repeats the cycle. Often, he has new insights to add when he returns.

"A memory technique that works well for me is to memorize in chucks (for example, one third or one half of a note page at a time)" a student at Brown University explained. "I will memorize a chunk and then do something to distract myself like throwing a ball against the wall. This distraction is important because it takes my mind off of what I was studying for a few minutes. Then, I go back and recall a chunk. I do this for chunks within a page, and then pages themselves. I have been able to recall anywhere from 50 to 150 pages of notes using this system."

In Bed: "I internalize information to be memorized by referring back to it in my mind," a student at the California Institute of Technology said. "I'll repeat the information when I'm in bed ready to sleep without referencing materials. In the morning, I reference what I could not remember, and I will typically not forget it."

In the Morning: A student at the University of Illinois at Chicago said that when he needs to memorize something, he gets up early in the morning when his mind is fresh and devotes a chunk of time to memorizing. He reads what has to be memorized and then tries to repeat it without looking. He is not satisfied even if he gets it on that day. He repeats the process daily.

Write It: "When I am trying to memorize something," a student at the University of Cincinnati offered, "I read one small section at a time. I cover the section with my hand and recite what I remember of that small section. If there is any part of the section that I do not remember as I recite, I write the part that I did not remember on scrap paper. As I recite the section again, I include the parts that I did not remember; sometimes, I only recite the parts that I did not remember. Then, I move on to the next section. I continue this process of reciting, writing parts that I did not remember on scrap paper, and reciting the section again all of the way through to the end of my notes."

Type It: Some find it helpful to re-type their lecture notes. "Once I was putting together on-line lecture notes for a class web site," a student at Harvard University said. "I would take notes by hand in class. Later that day, I would type the notes on a computer and upload them to the class web site. I ended up knowing that material probably better than the material in any other class I've taken and I only spent minimal time reviewing my notes before finals. The on-line notes I typed were meant to help everyone but I think I benefited the most. Typing helped me retain a lot."

A student at the University of Texas at El Paso types notes with no spaces and very small letters. The typing is done for mental imprinting at the time. However, the typed notes are not kept for future review. A student at the University of California at Los Angeles reads a certain amount of text and types out what he remembers. Then he goes back, determines what he did not remember of the section, and types that specific part. He continues with this through to the end of his notes. Here too, the typing is done temporarily for mental imprinting at the time.

Note Cards: Many people use note cards (index cards or flashcards). "I'm a math major," a student at the University of California at Davis said. "For every formula or concept I need to memorize, I make one small flashcard. Having the formulas on cards also makes it easier to find the formulas later." An anonymous student cited, "I write important formulas, definitions, and concepts on note cards." Some students place a question or key word on one side of the card and the answer or a matching phrase on the other side of the card. For foreign language courses, one strategy is to draw a picture on one side of the card and the foreign word on the other side. There is an association between the picture and the foreign word without the interference of English words.

"The key to the effective memorization of the facts is the repetition of a few cards at a time," a student at the University of California at Davis proposed. A student at Brunel University starts with five cards and continually adds five cards at a time. Another student at the University of California at Davis first puts ten flashcards in his stack and continually adds three at a time. A student at Texas Agricultural and Mechanical University thumbs through his stack of note cards periodically in those few minutes of spare time between classes, while walking, or while bored at lunch or work. A student at Auburn University School of Pharmacy reviews cards each night before going to sleep. Some people get copies of old examinations and make flashcards from the questions and answers on these old examinations.

Post-it Notes: "I like to invest in post-it notes," a student at Princeton University said. "While I am learning the information, I write down the main topics on post-it notes. For example, for biology, I write down the names of specific experiments. For history, I write down specific events. I carry these post-it notes with me. Every now and then, I flip through them and tell myself everything that I can about the topic. I place post-it notes for topics I don't know well on the wall in front of my desk to make sure I continually think about them." "Once," a student at Hampton University explained, "I stumbled upon a word whose definition I did not know. I looked it up in my dictionary. I wrote the word and its definition on a post-it note; I stuck the post-it note on the wall in my line of vision. The repetitiveness of seeing it forced me to remember it. Now, this is my favorite memory technique."

Just the Mnemonics: A student at Columbia University pointed out that he schedules time to review just the mnemonics. He said that if you know the mnemonics well, everything else will come back to you easily.

8C.32 Use the Same Numbers

A student at Mississippi State University pointed out that "People are frequently asked to assign a password for such things as computer accounts, bank accounts, school registration, and Internet sites. They may require different lengths (for example, four to eight digits). One can easily forget some of them if they are not used for quite a while. My strategy is to remember a ten-digit password. If anyone needs a four-digit password, I give him the last four digits of my magic password. If anyone needs seven digits, that person will get the last seven. In this way, I never have password problems with any system."

8C.33 Images

A student at the University of Colorado at Denver said that for physics and engineering subjects, he draws a picture of the problem. He imagines what happens in three-dimensional space. He uses physical intuition and visualizes the rotation of the objects in space. Sometimes he uses his pens and pencils as models. He translates algorithmic learning into graphic visualization. A student at the University of Tulsa imagines writing words or concepts that he needs to memorize on a blackboard. Another student, at the University of California at Los Angeles, draws a funny figure for each item that he learns. Associating funny images with what he is learning helps him remember it.

8C.34 Say It Out Loud or Act it Out

Comments included the following two: "I find that if I repeat whatever I am trying to memorize out loud, it is more likely to stay in my head"; "If you were to pop in on me, you would be quite amused. I act out what I am learning. In my experience, the more I get involved, the better I learn."

8C.35 Play Games

"To study for the first examination in one of my classes," a student at Auburn University said, "a classmate of mine and I had fun making obscure connections between protist names in order to help us remember them. For example, the components of the term, 'Pyrrhophyta (Dinoflagellates)' together might suggest a fire that caused the toxic red tide. Red and fire went together, and made it easier to remember. We were having fun joking around with the names, and this made it that much easier to learn. My score on that examination was perfect after the instructor adjusted it two points due to bad questions. For the second and third examinations, I did the same thing with a different friend, and my scores out of 100, were 100 and 102, respectively. The more times I went over the information either alone, or more often, with a friend, the better I knew it, and was able to recall it for examinations. I was also very relaxed about my performance. The study times were to learn information but they were also just some fun time to spend with a friend. After the test was turned in to the instructor, I also completely stopped worrying about it...."

8C.36 Give Him What He Wants?

Some students believe in asking the instructor what he wants to see in an assignment and then simply giving it to him. As one anonymous student insisted, "The world is a biased place. People in decision-making positions want what they want." Other students believe in attending to the instructor's expectations but not to his personal preferences. Some believe that the instructor will be fair if the student presents a point of view that is different from the instructor's point of view. A student at Ohio University suggested the idea of adjusting to each teacher's style.

8C.37 Presentations

Sometimes students must give presentations on a predefined topic to a class. The student can show initiative and ask the instructor if he or she can give a presentation to the class on a topic. A student at the University of Oregon advised, "Refrain from reading the presentation directly from a paper. Pick words or phrases that cue you into each section or subsection. Create a wild story that includes these words. Remember the story. Then you can glide through the presentation without having to read it. Give the presentation with enthusiasm and smiles to help classmates and the instructor get excited about the topic."

"Mentally prepare for possible interruptions that can take place before, during or after the presentation. These might include questions or agendas of other people. If a student wants to prove that he knows more about an item than you, compliment the student's contribution, explain why you think it is important, and then move on to the next item."

Think of the audience as members of your family. You are simply having a nice conversation with them. Do not think of them as people who are staring at you and scrutinizing your every move. This is YOUR world. If anything, perhaps you are the one staring at them and scrutinizing their moves.

8C.38 Monitor Your Progress

Some students monitor their own progress to correct mistakes as they occur and to increase the efficiency of their work. Some reserve one or more dividers in their binders for this purpose.

SECTION 8D: COMMON WRITING ASSIGNMENTS

Many students offered additional advice for writing assignments. These are presented below.

Title: Grab the reader's attention right away with an intriguing title. Choose a title that makes the reader curious and excited about what is on the pages to come. Some students like to wait until they have written most of the paper before choosing a title, and/or completing an introduction to ensure that the title and introductions are true reflections of the contents of the final paper.

"After the title," a student at the University of Wisconsin-Eau Claire suggested, "start your paper with a profound quotation on the subject, for example, from a famous leader." Quotations can be added to other parts of the paper. For example, some students like to end a paper with a powerful quotation. Some online resources for quotations, dictionaries, thesauri, and encyclopedias are listed in Appendix C.

Students had a number of suggestions for the format of writing assignments. Check the syllabus or other instructions about formatting requirements before getting started. One strategy is to use formats that are formally used in the field of study even if such formats are not required. Another is to use a larger number of categories than are required. For example, the student can include what is referred to as "front matter." This includes title page, preface, quotation page, table of contents, abstract, executive summary, dedication page, acknowledgments page, author's note, about the author, how to contact the author, biographical sketch, forward (for example from a local official or expert), list of tables, list of graphs, list of figures, list of displays, index of abbreviations, and/or equipment used. At the end of the paper, the student can include both a discussion and a conclusion. "End matter" can be added too. This includes author's reflection, afterward, appendix, supplements, endnotes, credit page, bibliography, reference, glossary, and/or index.

Topics: The teacher might have great ideas for topics since she knows what has been done in the past, what has worked, what does not work, and what fits well within the parameters of the class. One option is to simply ask the teacher about possible topics. It is also useful to pick a topic that you really like. If you like it, you are more likely to do a great job. One strategy is to pick a topic that you are actively curious about. Examples may include topics that you have seen in a newspaper, magazine, radio, television, or Internet. Some online resources for searching newspapers, magazines, journals, and their archives are listed in Appendix B. The student can read some basic information about the topic in a general reference like an encyclopedia or a computer catalogue. Once the student has found a topic, he can learn about the topic's subcategories and consider combining the subcategories into questions or solid statements to define a thesis statement for the paper. If there are two or three basic arguments that can be made on the topic or subtopic, the student can briefly list the pros and cons of each on scrap paper and then choose the one that has the most support.

It can be useful to write an outline of the essay's putative structure, showing the categories and subcategories to be included in the essay in an order that is consistent with the order in the thesis sentence. An outline can increase the chance that appropriate things are included and that the information will be presented in an appropriate sequence. It also creates a tentative table of contents. It is normal for an outline to be changed as new ideas come up in the process. Subsections can be changed, moved, replaced, or added.

Some students take a different approach. They do not write an outline for the paper right away. Instead, they first let the writing take its own natural course. Then, they read through everything that they have written, allowing an intriguing outline to come into view on its own. For example, a student at Stanford University writes a draft very fast from beginning to end, placing what comes to her mind on paper without regard to correctness of information, grammar, or spelling. If in the process of writing this first draft she gets stuck, she simply writes "I don't know," "I'm stuck," or why she thinks she is stuck, and then she keeps quickly writing to the end of the draft. The idea here is that her "subconscious" already has a sense of the direction and underlining structure of the paper; it simply needs a chance to run its course and get it out on paper quickly in a natural order. When her "conscious mind" goes back and reads what has been written, it identifies what is often a unique and exciting outline embedded in the original draft.

Students gather detailed information for their papers from many sources. These include: traditional card catalogs; citation, periodical, bibliographical, and book review indexes; library specialty collections; computer catalogs and indexes; computer-linked libraries and network information sources; CD-ROMS; Internet searches; bibliographies of relevant books or periodicals; and microfiche.

Many schools have online public access catalogs that allow the student to search not only the library's catalogs but also its specialty CD-ROMS, its subscription electronic databases with partial or complete texts of newspaper and periodical text articles, and the Internet. In some cases, all of these options are available at one or more computer terminal in the library. At such computer terminals, students can often perform searches using search criteria like subject, word, author, title, call number, language, publication type, publisher, year of publication, synonyms, asterisks, quotation marks, and/or Boolean operators like "and," "or," and "not." Combining search criteria can often increase the chance of isolating the specific information of interest. Many schools allow the convenience of remote access to their computer databases, so the student can access it from home or a dormitory. Become an expert on what your school library has available to save time and increase research efficiency. Consider references within references. Use tools on the Internet that journalists use, like those listed in Appendix G.

Incorporate unusual but relevant primary sources, like exerts from diaries, poetry, speeches, autobiographies, period publications, period correspondence, congressional or governmental debates, sessions, hearings, or laws. Some web sites that list primary sources are given in Appendix D. Consider including inexpensive primary research. Examples include: interviewing local officials in person, over the telephone, or via the Internet and including their responses in the paper; conducting a survey of friends, classmates, or other relevant local small group of people; and analyzing publicly available data. The author can create a simple experiment and describe first-hand experience with the topic. Some resources for simple experiments are listed in Appendix E.

"A common mistake is to over try an essay," a student at Stanford University said. "This happened to me in English classes. I would spend so much time planning and gathering background information that I would end up writing the paper the night before and not have enough time to revise it." Don't do it all or most of it all at once. Pace yourself. Do a certain number of paragraphs, sections, or hours each day. Only seek, take notes, or otherwise store information that is specific to your thesis statement or thesis question. Each time, before you read something or write a note on or about something, ask "Does this directly address my thesis question?" If it doesn't, don't do it. You can save time by coding information that you gather towards specific parts of your outline.

It is important to do particularly well on those parts of the writing assignment that you are sure the reader will actually read. As a student at Ohio University commented, "Sometimes a faculty member's work load or time constraints may affect his or her ability to accurately grade assignments. For example, a Management Information Systems faculty member commented that he only had two weeks to grade eighty term papers, eighty final examinations, and twenty team projects. Realistically, he probably would not be able to read and accurately score all of those assignments. This meant that when grading the term paper, he would probably read the executive summary, introduction, maybe the first couple of pages, and the conclusion. He would most likely skim through the remainder of the paper. This was an opportunity to excel by placing extra effort into these parts of the term paper."

Other suggestions from students included varying the length of sentences and paragraphs, and using simple (and clear) language. One standard is to describe one idea at a time (e.g., one idea per paragraph). Clarity can be increased by describing what something is but also taking a moment to briefly point out what it is not. Support general observations with specific data. Include succinct examples and analogies to establish credibility and coherence. Be precise. Describe the best and worst case scenarios. Refrain from repeating words and phrases; this can bore or irritate the reader. Remove unnecessary words. They take up space and attention from other words. They can also reduce credibility. For example, the term, "intelligent" is more credible than "very intelligent." "Reliable" is more credible than "absolutely reliable." If you can, include color illustrations, pictures, maps, and accompanying legions. Some online resources for images and maps are listed in Appendix F. Consider describing circumstances and characters in action or using active metaphors to make the reading more exciting.

The reader should be able to understand why points have been made and issues raised. There should be clear links between points. If you are going to argue in favor of the teacher's (or author's) views, try to do so better than the teacher (or author) by using information learned in journals, other classes, and life experiences.

Conclusion: A common mistake is for a student to do a great job on the introduction and body of the paper but end with a short conclusion. The student is tired and wants to get it over with or simply runs out of time. One message is to run all of the way through the finish line. Deliberately over-extend the conclusion of the paper. This will give the reader the impression that the student is serious and only stopped because he was required to do so.

For the conclusion (or concluding section), the student might restate the original thesis statement or theme. He can summarize or discuss the significance of each section of the paper. What light did the information in the body of the paper bring to the past, present, or future? What effect did or does the subject, the issue, the process, or the process of doing this paper have on the writer, other individuals, groups, regions, or society? What research projects can be done in the future to address this? How might it be done? What improvements in equipment, methods, or goals could be made? What results might you expect to find? Which results would be the most meaningful? Consider reserving some of the spicy things that students would normally place in the body of the essay for the concluding section of the paper to make it more intense. In the bibliography, include works cited as well as relevant works that were not cited in the paper to make the bibliography more complete and to make it longer. Software programs that can facilitate the creation of a bibliography include End Note and Reference Master.

As you review the work, ask yourself some of the following questions. Did I answer the specific questions set out in the instructions? Did I achieve the objectives described in the introduction of my paper? Did I adequately support the thesis sentence? Am I happy with the integrity and the quality of my judgments? Is this work convincing? Did I demonstrate an understanding of the material? Is there any part of this that I can make more coherent? Can I strengthen the argument by rearranging the elements of certain sentences or choosing more specific references in my descriptions? Are there additional links that I can recognize or that I can make? Are there any finishing touches that I can add to this that an A student will not?

Spelling and Grammar: Some papers have great content but have spelling and grammatical errors. The grader can become irritated and arrive at an early negative impression; from there, things can go down hill. Like everyone else, graders don't like to be irritated. Make the reading a pleasant experience for the graders, from beginning to end, and they will respond to the work in a pleasant way. "After you have done the spelling and grammar check options which come with most word processing programs," a student at Indiana University of Pennsylvania said, "it is important to go over the paper manually to catch things that such programs may not identify like appropriate uses of 'to' and 'too.'" There are also some mistakes that can be more readily seen on paper than on a computer screen. "As you check for grammar and spelling, pretend that it is a game," a student at Yale University advised. "You get points each time you find the slightest mistake in your own paper."

In addition to correct spelling and grammar, there should also be appropriate use of documentation style. The most popular documentation style is MLA (Modern Language Association) parenthetical style. Other popular documentation styles include MLA footnote style, MLA endnote style, and APA (American Psychological Association) documentation style. Online resources for grammar and documentation style are listed in Appendix C. If your documentation style is not correct, at least make it consistent.

Show Others: Have at least one other person whose judgment you trust to read the paper. Each person looks at the world from a slightly different angle and may recognize something that someone else does not. Some students have a peer-editing circle. They exchange papers for review at scheduled times. Some find that this keeps them from procrastinating.

Sometimes the advisor's suggestions are wonderful but the advisor has not himself done a complete literature search on the specific subtopic and may not be completely aware of certain brick walls that may await you there. Double-check everything.

Consider the following questions for yourself and for your advisor. Does your department have access to all of the equipment that you will need to effectively address the topic of your research? If the department does have the equipment, will you be allowed to have access to it as often as you need it? Can you get along with the other people in the laboratory where you will be working? Would you benefit more by working with others who are working on similar projects or with more space to yourself? Can the research question be answered in the time allotted for the dissertation or in the period of time that you hope to graduate? Is your topic too broad? Can this project lead to a well-defined set of results? Can your budget cover all of the work that will be needed? Ask these questions before starting. Some students make the mistake of waiting until they have been doing their thesis for one or more years before asking these simple but critical questions. Do not begin the research until you are personally convinced and each main step makes logical sense to you.

Choose a thesis advisor that you get along with and whose biases are not in conflict with your thesis. The more comfortable you feel with your mentor, the easier it is to take guidance, accept criticism, and make progress. Make sure that your mentor has a sincere interest in the subject of your thesis; otherwise, he might not put forth a genuine effort. Ask senior students and faculty about the advisor's record with previous students. Did the previous students have a good experience, complete their thesis in a reasonable period of time, or complete it at all? What percentage of his students completed the thesis? Does he share credit for shared work? Is he available on a regular basis? Is his reputation and area of expertise conducive to your future employment plans? Will he assist you in establishing connections with other experts in the field and post-graduate placements? In addition to speaking to others in the department, some students acquire information by searching a citation index. The three major ones are Science Citation Index, Social Sciences Citation Index, and Arts and Humanities Citation Index. A citation index can indicate an author's publications. It can also show who and how many people have made reference to the author's publication. Another resource is "Essential Science Indicators," produced by the Institute for Scientific Information. It is a web product which includes analyses of research performance and data for ranking scientists. Some students acquire additional information about the putative advisor by reading his publications, attending his seminars, or taking one or more of his classes early in the process. Once the student has chosen someone, both parties need to clarify their expectations and needs. Clarify how frequently you will meet, what you expect to get out of each meeting, what will be reviewed or scrutinized at each stage, schedules, and response times. This is important because students and advisors are individuals; each has his and her own perception of what these things should be. A student might expect a response in two weeks but an advisor might assume that five weeks is comfortable. Different and unclarified expectations are common sources of conflict.

It is also important to be careful about who you pick for your thesis committee. Investigate the habits of potential members of your thesis committee by speaking with others who have experience with them. If one person on the committee has a bad habit of holding things up or being overly dogmatic about his philosophies, it can be a perpetual problem. It is also important not to include members who do not get along with each other. Their battles with each other can inhibit the progress of the dissertation.

"Be organized," a student at the University of California at Los Angeles said. "Divide the work and set a tentative schedule and deadline for each part. Check against it often. Be disciplined. Get up early in the morning just like you did when you were taking classes. So many Ph.D. students get up late and work for a few hours. They don't take advantage of all of the time available to them in the day." Some students like to reserve a particular day in the week to read articles in specific journals that are relevant to the research topic. This allows the student to keep up-to-date. One student at Columbia University brings along a stack of index cards. For each significant article that she finds, she fills out an index card with a title of the relevant section of her thesis, reference information, and a brief description of the parts of the article that she finds to be significant. Using index cards in this way prevents her from writing too much for each article, keeps the information organized, and facilitates consideration for future incorporation into specific parts of the dissertation. Some students photocopy the abstract and/or other relevant parts of significant articles and have a sorting system for storage.

As you do research, write and date everything in a research notebook. Write empirical data but also your thoughts, questions, and frustrations at the time. Some students code these different categories in the notebook as they write. Some have one notebook for empirical data and another for their thoughts and questions. Although thoughts may seem scrambled and irrelevant at the time, later you'll find that there was a reason why you asked those questions. Fifty percent of the things that you have written will end up in your final thesis. You will know which fifty percent later in the process. Periodically read through your notes and code information that seems significant for parts of the thesis at the time.

As time passes, you can transfer relevant information from your notebooks into the document that will develop into your thesis. "You will see once you have enough research together that you will write the thesis much faster than you think," a student at the University of Southern California insisted. "The hardest part seems to be the start." Another student, at Cambridge University, said, "It helps me to try to think and write during most of the process rather than trying to do all of the thinking first and then 'write up' at the end."

One effective format for a dissertation is the following: (A) Introduction. The introduction can be "completed" last since the student will not know the results of the research until it is over. (B) Background. Here, the student describes the history of the topic. Sometimes the background is its own section; in other cases, it's a subsection of the introduction.
(C) Current State of the Art. Describe, for example, the three or four main lines of thinking or strategies in present day research on the topic. This section also describes the pros and cons of each of the main ideas.
(D) The Unanswered Question. Describe the question that remains unanswered, why it is important to ask this question, and why it is important to attempt to answer it. (E) Original Contributions. Describe how you attempted to answer the question and your findings.
(F) Conclusion. Summarize each section of the dissertation; sum up your original contributions to the topic; review the remaining limitations; and suggest future research. This six-step format for a dissertation is one format. However, there are many different ways to organize a dissertation. Once the student has determined a topic, he can ask his thesis advisor to show him some models of how topics in this area of study can be done. The student can pick a model that is conducive to his writing, research, and personal style. A model can be useful but the student can vary from it and speak with his own voice. The writing is directed towards an audience; in this case, the audience is the thesis committee.

If the student does not get the research results that he originally expected or wanted, that's fine. The student might write a thesis which attempts to explain the reasons why the research results are negative. A negative result does not necessarily mean that the student has done something wrong. There are often legitimate reasons why research results are negative. Often, it is because it tells a truth of a pathway or opens up windows to future avenues of consideration and assessment on the topic. The information can allow investigators to undergo a process of elimination. Thus, negative results are often valuable and can be treated as such. There are students who have written the entire dissertation describing a negative result and the student's perception of its significance. It should also be noted that a thesis does not have to solve a problem; it can explore it instead. A thesis can describe models, complexities, barriers, and contradictions of an issue in ways that are more detailed and up-to-date than others have in the past. Such exploration is science too; the information can be useful for the student and other scientists who study the topic.

Some parts of the thesis will take longer than others. As one anonymous student said, "It took me 10% of the time to write the first 90% of my thesis (because much of the first part was a description and discussion of historical data leading up to my research). It took the remaining 90% of the time to write the last 10% of my thesis." If the student must meet with the advisor and has not progressed, the student can simply explain to the advisor why he thinks he has not progressed; perhaps the advisor can help. The student can also get through difficulty by breaking the task into small manageable pieces and addressing one piece at a time. If a piece is publishable, some students like to go ahead and write an article for the piece for publication in a workshop, conference proceeding, or journal. The process of writing articles for publication can establish nice summaries for parts of the dissertation.

Make the reading and analysis of the dissertation easy and convenient for the reader. If the reader has a pleasant experience, she is more likely to respond in a pleasant way. If the dissertation is long, remind the reader of where she is and why she is there, so she doesn't get lost in the details. This can be furthered by incorporating extra titles in the paper, using colored sheets between sections, or using labeled dividers between sections of the dissertation. In subsections, present points that support your argument in the order of most important to least important or strongest point to weakest point. Avoid politically incorrect comments. In the bibliography, include papers published by your advisor and/or members of the thesis committee. In the appendix, include data that directly supports your thesis argument but would otherwise interfere with smooth descriptions if it were placed in the body of the dissertation. Use the documentation style requirements of your department and/or university.

Accept the fact that much of what you considered over the course of research will not end up in the final thesis. There is not enough room in the thesis to include everything. There will be plenty of time after graduation to pursue additional questions that you have accumulated over time.

Thesis Police: A student at Hamilton College had a group of fellow students that she referred to as the "thesis police." As she stated, "Their job was to ask me as frequently as they desired how my thesis was progressing and whether I had put in a daily minimum of hours. I was obligated to answer both honestly and graciously. Although this was not always easy, it helped so much! I'm not sure that I could have made it alone." Some students create an organized group of students in the department. The students meet at regular scheduled times and exchange their papers for review. Some departments have established student thesis review groups and students sign up if and when they are ready.

Periodically, the student will meet with the thesis committee to review the student's progress. The student can give an oral presentation of what he has done so far, what he is currently doing, and what he plans to do in the future. He is advised to answer short questions with short answers. Long questions can be dealt with by answering one part at a time, starting with the part that the student knows best. If the student does not know an answer, he can consider the possibility that he knows some fraction of the answer and present that part. Sometimes, committee members ask questions that are outside of the scope of the student's thesis statement. The student can politely remind the member of the specificity of the thesis mission.

Outside of the scheduled committee meetings, the student might take the initiative to make appointments with each individual member of the thesis committee. Each member will know that the student is including the member in the thought process. Ideally, the student will have picked members that are experts in different aspects of his thesis topic. He gains the benefit of the member's expertise. The student can ask each member rigorous questions about parts of the thesis that correspond to the member's area of expertise. In addition to improving the quality of the thesis, this can mean that by the time the student gets to his thesis defense, the hardest questions that are relevant will have already been answered by the same people who would otherwise ask the student these questions at the thesis defense. This is the principle of "asking them before they ask you."

It is also wise to ask senior students and faculty in the department about the historical structure and contents of the thesis defense in the department. In some cases, the student is allowed to establish an agreement with the thesis committee about the type and/or range of questions to be fielded at the thesis defense; this helps to focus the preparation. After thinking about basic questions in the range, think about how elements relate to each other. It is also useful to arrange a mock thesis defense with other students in the department asking hard questions.

SECTION 8F: ARTS

Some students offered advice for the arts:

(A) Master the Fundamentals: For example, an artist who paints can learn the fundamental design approaches and the appropriate conditions for their applications. She might learn fundamental rendering principles like that of rendering the parts of a painting from its light parts through to its dark parts. This is exemplified in the following four-step series: (1) sketch the basic pattern in pencil; (2) apply base colors; (3) add the darker colors and shading; and (4) apply outlining in black. The artist might learn fundamentals of color theory like the concept of color pair. Color pairs include yellow and purple; red and green; and orange and blue. When using one color, adding a bit of its complementary color can create realism and depth in the painting. Another fundamental is color repeat: Once a color is chosen, it can be used in more than one place in the picture to create a sense that elements belong together in a scene.

A musician might become proficient in the fundamentals of his instrument by knowing the scales of his instrument well, including high and low notes that other students pay little attention to, and by learning how to play notes in more than one way with different fingering. A thorough knowledge of fundamentals provides the person with more options and therefore more flexibility when difficulty arises. For example, if a pianist forgets or falters on a chord, he might at least ensure that the notes fall into the right scale because of his knowledge of fundamentals.

(B) Rehearse Elements in Isolation and Together: A pianist might separately rehearse treble cleft notes, base cleft notes, transitions, areas of difficulty, other elements, and then play them together. An actor can rehearse the words, gestures, characterizations, form, style, ensemble, atmosphere, and transitions of the performance in isolation, perform some of the components together, and all of them together. A singer might practice breathing, rhythm, melody, tempo, dictation, tone, pitch, and volume in isolation, and together.

(C) Rehearse Related Forms: An example is a singer who also practices singing slightly above and slightly below her designated pitch. She can rehearse whistling or humming the song. A saxophonist might rehearse the finger movements, in some cases with the saxophone in hand, and in other cases without it.

(D) Mentally Rehearse: A musician might read through the score without his instrument, think about each note or chord individually and think about how each should sound. He might think through a few measures at a time, stop, and then play these few measures. He can do the opposite: play a few measures at a time, stop, and then mentally repeat the measures. A dancer might mentally rehearse individual or groups of movements before actually dancing the movements.

Mentally Tune-in to the Immediate Environment: A flute player can perceive her instrument, its keys, and its sound as natural extensions of herself. An artist can think of his brush as a natural extension of his hands. A singer can tune-in to his environment by thinking of the emotional significance of the lyrics. Live the lyrics. Be the lyrics. This can apply to acting. An actor might perceive her immediate environment as a dynamic place. "Each character and object in the atmosphere has its own energy and continuous life that is real. The actor can tune-in to these images, experience them, affect them, influence them, make them significant, and convey them to the audience."

Mental rehearsal can also include learning to concentrate. Concentration might be increased by describing and asking questions about individual details of the items to be focused upon.

(E) Remain Loose: One suggestion was to keep muscles relaxed, particularly those muscles that are not directly involved in the performance. To reduce rigidity, an artist can stretch the muscles that will be involved, before and after the performance. He can also think of his body and his instrument as flexible weightless entities that can adjust to the subtleties of the performance.

(F) Identify Details: Look for little things that you may not have detected before and study their details.

(G) Continuously Refine the Work: Push it to or beyond a professional level. Think about conceptual, formal, theoretical, and experimental boundaries; then go beyond them.

(H) Instinct: One approach is to practice the art or the piece over time until it feels instinctual. Over long periods of time, instinct might provide the artist with a sense of when it is okay to break certain rules to find a higher standard.

(I) Exchange Information with Others: Communicate with others about what you have learned and pay attention to what they have learned. Allow them to scrutinize your work and listen attentively to their comments. Their responses may open up new avenues of thought and opportunity. They might see something wonderful in work that you thought was a disaster. Observe and study the details of the work of people who you look up to. Search for the specific reasons why these individuals are the best. There is an underlining pattern to their success and you might find it by questioning yourself to the answer.

(J) Learn the History and Culture: Learning how the piece developed over time and the factors that influenced it can provide further insight. Applying this information and immersing oneself in the culture at many levels can increase the authenticity of the final product. An example of this is an actor who spends time living the life (or components of the life) of the person whom he/she is to portray.

(K) Landmarks: An artist might draw guidelines in pencil before drawing an object. He can use the rule of fourths or the rule of thirds. For example, in the case of the rule of thirds, the canvas is divided into three horizontal sections and three vertical sections. This creates a preliminary grid for the placement of objects in the picture. Another example is a musician who identifies four or five pleasant landmarks in the musical score. He can think of the pleasant landmarks, one at a time, as he makes his way through the song. Artists who must look towards an audience during performance might pick three or four physical landmarks in the auditorium. The artist might continuously rotate between these landmarks or use specific landmarks for specific parts of the performance. A landmark can be virtually anything. It can be an object, part of an object, a specific person, a group of people, parts of groups of people like the hair or the foreheads of audience members, a shape, a mark, a word, a sound, a site, a smell, or a gesture.

(L) Draw from Personal Experience: An example is an actor who brings out an emotion or other characteristic by thinking about a related experience or related issue in his own life. Another example is a musician who writes a song and draws from the experience of a relationship.

(M) Create Your Own Style: There are many subjective ways to do this. One suggestion was, as described above, to draw from personal experience. Use your own ideas, emotions, mannerisms, and expressions. Combine them. Another suggestion was to choose a small limited space, create a simple attractive pattern in this limited space, and then add one element at a time until it develops into a masterpiece: An example is a pianist who picks one octave and one to five measures as his limited space; creates a simple attractive melody in this one to five measures; adds notes to the original notes to create attractive chords; and adds one element, instrument, or voice at a time to the notes in these first five measures. He has now created five measures worth of excellence! He might start the next five measures in the same way. This is only one example of the concept of building a masterpiece one step at a time. However, there are MANY different ways to accomplish this with excellence.

Some students suggested methods of improvisation: One suggestion was to practice the work of people who are great but allow mistakes to occur. Go with the mistakes and see where they take you. If you are a musician and think that a quarter note sounds better than a half note there, go with it. As you make small or large changes, ask yourself if your chosen alternative is more attractive or less attractive to you. Over time, your conscious study of specific elements that are attractive to you can help you to find distinction. A student at Columbia University stated, "Arnie Berle's book does a great job of describing ways to improvise. These include the following: Switch the location of one or more elements in the same measure. Take something that would normally be played on the upbeat and play it instead on the downbeat. Divide the notes. For example, divide a quarter note into two half notes or vise versa. Omit notes of the melody in some measures. Just before specific notes in the melody, consider adding a note that is one of the following: (1) A half-step below the note in the melody. (2) A full-step above and in the same scale of the note in the melody. This strategy is simple and effective."

(N) Reverse Your Perception: Do not perceive the members of the audience as scrutinizing you and your every move. Instead, recognize that this is YOUR world. You might perceive yourself as the one who is scrutinizing them and their every move, if this is to be the case. Perhaps they are the ones to be apprehensive.

(O) Believe Yourself: Believe yourself to increase the standard and the chance that others will believe in your work too.

(P) Manage Outcomes: "Be open-minded to but not stuck on outcomes."

SECTION 9: BEFORE TEST

9.1 What Will It Cover?

Always find out what a test will cover. You don't want to spend hours, days or weeks laboring over more than what is needed.

9.2 Review

"During the term," a student at the University of California at Berkeley said, "each time I review my notes, I rewrite them, condensing them down to successively smaller sizes. Sometimes, this includes a cheat sheet. One or two weeks before a test is the time to review already clarified, shrunken, and learned material. If you run out of time, you already know it. If you have one of those teachers who keeps assigning reading all of the way into the last day before the test, it is okay. Just make sure that the material preceding these last few days is clarified, shrunken, and learned. Then, you'll only have to read through the material of the last day(s) at the end."

"I start the final review for tests one to four weeks before my tests," a student at Louisiana State University said. "If there is only one test, I'll typically start the final review one week before the test. If it is a hard class, I might start two weeks before the test. If there are many tests scheduled close together, I'll start as early as three to four weeks before the first test. I divide the amount that needs to be reviewed by the number of days I set for the final review. For example, if I start one week before the test, I'll divide the total amount into seven parts, doing one part on each of the seven days leading to the test. Alternatively, I'll divide it by six days and leave the seventh day for unresolved issues that remain. Reviewing the material in parts lets it sink in better and there is less stress." Some students divide the review time up amongst their classes based on the level of difficulty or impact on final grades. For example, if a class is twice as difficult or if the test will have twice the impact on grades, a student might allocate twice as much time during the final review period for it.

A student at Columbia University asserted, "I use Gordon Green's approach. I correct or rewrite my notes in the afternoon after each class. This is my first review. In the week before a test, I review my notes three more times: First, I breeze through the notes, not worrying about details. The second time, a couple days later, I spend more time on details. The third and final time is the day before the test. That's it! I go to sleep early the night before the test."

Order: Some students study for tests in the order that the tests will be given. Others review in the reverse order than the tests will be given. A benefit of the reverse approach is that the student will have studied for the first test soon before it starts, providing a good start on the series. Near the end of the series, as energy runs out, the student will have already reviewed for these last tests.

"If I have four exams scheduled for the same day," a student at Baylor University explained, "in the preceding two to three weeks, I'll switch back and forth in my final review. I might review one subject for an hour, switch to reviewing a second subject for an hour, and then switch to reviewing another subject for an hour. I switch in one to three-hour intervals, depending on the circumstance." Switching back and forth keeps the review process interesting, keeps the student energetic, and gains mileage on each of the subjects that need to be reviewed. Some students take it a step further and switch in a proportional way. For example, the student can review for a class that is twice as difficult for two hours, before switching to review for a less difficult class for one hour.

A student at the University of Cincinnati advised, "Review in accordance with the test format." A student at North Carolina State University stated, "A professor that likes multiple choice will need to be studied most carefully, as you need to understand his mindframe for phrasing answers that are similar (but he deems only one answer to be correct). Ones that have you do fill in's expect you to know their notes very well. Those that use multiple correct answers on multiple choice (like option 'e' that says 'a, b, and d are correct') expect you to know stuff they assigned in reading but never commented on." A student at the University of Cincinnati said, "Usually, the most important things to review are in the lecture notes. This is because most teachers prefer their views and emphasis over that of the text." "I review lecture notes, marked areas in the book, my answers to hard questions from the homework assignments and the back of each chapter, and my flashcards," a student at Columbia University said. Some students do odd numbered questions or random questions in the textbook as part of their preparation just before a test. One student at Harvard University likes to read all of the materials to be covered on the test one last time before the test so that she has a lot of information in her head at the time of the test.

"For myself," a student at Indiana University of Pennsylvania remarked, "I need to be alone in a quiet room." For some, the final review means a similar schedule but having a well-prepared friend grill them on the material.

Many students make the mistake of trying to learn the material for the first time in one long cram session just before a test. The review process can be further retarded for those students who left their notes unclarified during the term. Comments included the following: "Most courses demand much more than what one could ever accomplish in one night of cramming"; "Cramming fries out the brain. You put so much into the studying that you are mentally exhausted at test time; the mind goes blank"; "Cramming is overwhelming, mentally and physically draining, inefficient, and ultimately ineffective"; "It leaves you too frazzled to function the next morning"; "Cramming and pulling all-nighters work far less often than people claim."

9.3 The Night Before the Test

"If you can," a student at the University of Oregon suggested, "familiarize yourself with the test instructions and format beforehand so that you can save time during the test itself." For many students, the last thing they review before a test is a "cheat" sheet containing tricky stuff, formulas, units of measurement, and/or things to memorize. For some, the last look at their notes takes place the night before the examination.

"You may want to set a study deadline for when you will stop studying for the night," a student at Indiana University of Pennsylvania proposed. "If you do this, it helps to tell someone in your home what this time is and ask that person to alert you at this time so that you have some force involved. This way, you don't keep telling yourself, 'ten more minutes and then I'll stop.'"

"When I finish studying for the night," a student at the University of Illinois at Urbana-Champaign said, "I eat a bowl of ice cream and relax."

9.4 Sleep

"It may sound clichéd," a student at the University of Nevada at Reno admitted, "but a good night's sleep and a good breakfast really do help."

"Aim for eight hours of sleep the night before the test," a student at Indiana University of Pennsylvania said. "Sleep in comfortable pajamas and let yourself relax once you hit the sheets."

9.5 Morning of the Examination

For some students, the last look at the notes is in the morning. "I always study up until about a half an hour before the test," a student at Indiana University at Bloomington said. "Make sure that your schedule is completely clear around the time of the test so that you can deal with last minute problems," a student at Rutgers University advised. A student at North Carolina State University at Raleigh said, "Right before the exam, take at least one hour or more of no thinking about the exam. Then, give yourself fifteen minutes before the exam to think about it."

"If you usually wear a scent (like perfume, cologne, or a scented body wash) when you study or have class, wear the same fragrance for your examination," a student at Indiana University of Pennsylvania said. "Some research has linked the scent ties to helping test performance, possibly in jogging memory. The theory is that the more similar your test-taking conditions are to the conditions in which you learned and studied the material, the more you will be able to recall during the examination." A student at the University of Wisconsin-Eau Claire said that he always wears his lucky shirt to tests so that he can say that it was the shirt.

Some of the students suggested things to bring to the test. These included: two pencils; pencil sharpener; two similar pens; eraser; highlighters; blue books (if needed); scrap paper; white-out; calculator (if needed) and spare battery; a watch, timer, or clock; any allowed notes; any allowed books with bookmarks at important pages and a list of important tables on the inside front cover; tissue paper; and food. "When taking a test, it is important to pamper yourself," a student at the

University of Haifa in Israel said. "I bring two candy bars (ones with peanut-butter) and a can of coke." "When I'm taking a long test," a student at Harvard University said, "I like to have some candy on hand. Halfway or more into the examination, hopefully during a break or even during the test (discreetly) I eat it. After a couple of hours of essays or problems, any student will get tired and his mind may start to wander. I find that increasing my blood sugar as soon as I start running out of steam can help me refocus and keep on pace." "When I'm taking a test," a student at Brigham Young University offered, "I try to have something to munch on. My favorite are Black Forest Gummy Bears. They are quiet, last a long time, and provide a variety of flavors. When I get stressed out over a question that I don't know, I will think about gummy bears for a while. This distraction is not only relaxing, but it allows me to refocus when I face the question again."

9.6 In the Test Room

For some students, the last look at notes is in the test room. "I try to get to the examination early," a student at the University of Illinois at Urbana-Champaign said, "so that I can go over the information in the very room where the test will be administered. My reasoning behind these actions is based on a loose exaggeration of state dependence, the psychological concept that memory improves when learning and testing phases occur in the same emotional and physical setting. This refreshes your memory, and you'll find that everything comes flooding back in the exam room."

A student at Idaho State University said that she gets to the examination room early enough to accomplish three things. The first is to find a good seat. To her, this means a seat where the blackboard and the clock are in view, the lighting is good, and distracting students are not near her. The second is to glance over her notes one last time. The third is to relax for a moment by taking several slow deep breaths and concentrating on relaxing her whole body.

SECTION 10: DURING TEST

10.1 General Advice

Take two deep breaths before starting. Give yourself instructions throughout the test. Place your name on all relevant sheets. Consider writing acronyms, acrostics, formulas, lists or outlines that you have difficulty retaining on scrap paper or on the test itself (either next to relevant questions or all in one place); however, do not waste time writing information that you do not have difficulty retaining.

Scan through the test. Get a sense of the number of questions, distribution of points, and amount of space. Make a quick estimation of how much time you will have for each question if you don't already know. In your estimate, consider the possibility of more than one pass through the questions and revision at the end. The estimate does not have to be exact.

"I go through and do the easy questions first," a student at Stanford University said. Next, I do the medium-difficulty questions, and then the difficult questions. The easy questions build confidence and get the ball rolling. If you run out of time, you will have completed the ones that you know for sure and maximized the number of points." "As I go through questions," a student at the University of Florida said, "I mark each with '1,' '2,' or '3,' where '1' is the easiest and '3' is the most difficult type. I circle the questions that give me problems." Other coding schemes were described. "I use hearts, moons, and stars," a student at the University of Kentucky at Lexington said. "Hearts mean I am fairly certain I am correct but review is preferred; moons mean I have a little more doubt; and stars mean I am no more certain I am correct than a monkey would be."

Another strategy is to place a question mark next to questions that you are not sure of, and two question marks next to questions that you are REALLY unsure of. A student at the University of Michigan said, "I answer the objective questions first, and I do the subjective questions second because there is always something more that can be written in response to the subjective questions."

"Read the questions incredibly carefully and all of the way through," a student at Cambridge University advised. Individual words make a big difference in a question. Components of words like prefixes, roots, and suffixes also give information. "I once didn't read the last sentence of a problem in which we were to hook up all the lines in the computer," a student at the University of California at Davis confessed. "The last sentence said that not all lines were necessarily used. I had four lines that were unconnected when I got finished, and I couldn't figure out what to do with them, so I connected them anyway. If I had read the last sentence in the problem, I would have known that they were extra." "On essay questions," a student at City College of New York warned, "beware of straying off the actual examination questions when they differ from those you have posed to yourself in your preparation for the test. Meet exactly the requirements specified." A student at Stanford University said, "Answer the specific question that is asked (not any other question). Underline or circle key words in the question that tell you what to do." "Put yourself in the professor's shoes, ask why he is asking the question, and what type of answer" a student at Boston College suggested. "If the professor likes to go into every detail of everything in class, then, if you have to guess with all else being equal, the most specific answer is probably best." "Don't hesitate to ask for clarification on a question during the test," one anonymous student insisted. "There can be more than one interpretation and this can translate into a huge difference in grading. At the same time, don't read too much between the lines; take the question for what it is. There is not an agenda behind every word."

"While you are reading," a student at Indiana University of Pennsylvania proposed, "squeeze the meat of your hand between your thumb and index finger. For example, use your right thumb and any right finger (whichever is strongest—most likely the index finger or middle finger) to sandwich the skin between your left thumb and left index finger. I read somewhere that applying pressure in this way for ten seconds boots energy. At the very least, it gives your hands a workout break from strangling those number two pencils! During essay tests, I pause occasionally to mini-massage my hard-working hands and fingers while re-reading a draft or writing prompt."

Completely answer each question one at a time. If you get stuck on a question, mark it and move on, especially if it is worth as much as other questions. You can come back and finish it in the last round. Some students go ahead and spend a few seconds to throw out a quick educated guess before moving on, in case they don't have time to come back. A student at Rutgers University delineates the educated guess part of his answer from the part of his answer that he is sure of so that he can go directly to the right part when he comes back. A student at the Massachusetts Institute of Technology writes a note in the margin next to the question, indicating points of confusion or questions to think about when he comes back.

Don't be bothered if you get stuck on a question. It is natural to run into a couple of these even if you are well prepared. It's the nature of the beast. The road is not a straight line. Subsequent questions in the same test may give hints to the answer. The process of answering other questions can trigger the answer to previous questions. In some cases, it works in the other direction. Answers to earlier questions can facilitate the answers to later questions. "A previous problem in chemistry might have asked for the molecular weight of a certain compound and stoichiometry is used to get it," a student at Auburn University said. "Later in the test, the same reaction may be given as a prompt for another question. Using the ratios from the balanced reaction in the first question, it is easier to get the correct answer for the later question." If you cannot determine the answer to a particular question by the last pass, just write the most "relevant" information to gain as much partial credit as you can. "Make sure it is relevant though because professors usually don't care for 'brain-dumps,' as a professor of mine called them," a student at King's University College in Canada cautioned.

10.2 Essay Questions

"Save enough time for the essay questions since they tend to be worth more points," a student at the University of California at Berkeley said. Don't get carried away with one question or one paragraph and run out of time for the rest of the test. A student at Stanford University said, "Take a moment to think about the meaning of the key verb in the essay question. This will keep you on track. If you are asked to 'criticize' something, focus on the pros and cons of the issue. If you are asked to 'illustrate' something, give examples and/or analogies in your answer. If you are asked to 'narrate' something, present events in the order in which they occurred." A student at the University of Maine explained that "Many essay questions ultimately want you to address one or more of the following: who, what, when, where, why, or how. Consider keywords in the essay question that might direct you to one of these. For example, if a question asks you to EXPLAIN something, you might focus your response on the characteristics, HOW and WHY. If a question asks you to JUSTIFY something, you might focus your response on the characteristic, WHY."

A student at the University of California at Berkeley said, "I always write my answers to essay questions in pencil so that I can make changes without leaving nasty marks on the paper."

It is smart to draw a brief diagram, flow chart, or outline of what you will cover. Then all you have to do is follow it. An outline increases the chance that important categories and subcategories are included, that the essay is not too short or too long, and that the information will be presented in chronological order. "Don't just jump right in without writing an outline because you will miss some things, and possibly work your way to a conclusion in the middle of the essay," a student at Princeton University advised. "I try to pick a thesis and state it within the first three to four sentences of my essay," a student at Central Michigan University offered. "Next, I pick three to five points to discuss and thoroughly explain them." A student at Stanford University said, "In the first paragraph, list three or four major points in order of importance. Next, write about each point in that order."

"I always try to cite the lectures and the textbook as often as possible in my essays," a student at Central Michigan University said. "This shows the instructor that I was in class, paid attention, and read the text. Occasionally, an instructor marks me down for a lack of creativity or says something like, 'I know what the textbook says. I want to know what you know.' However, these comments from my instructors are rare."

Strategies used on homework assignments can also be used on tests. Focus on presenting one idea at a time. One idea per paragraph is one standard. Use simple, clear, and concise language. Describe what something is and possibly what it is not. Describing what something is not can provide some information when you don't know what it is. This is what some experts do. They admit that no one knows the true answer but pin-point what it is not or what it could not be; they get credit and praise for this information because it is more than nothing and often more than what anyone else knows. A student at the University of California at Los Angeles advised "To get through a difficult subsection use a three-point approach: Define a principle, give one or two examples, add a concluding sentence and then get on to your next subsection."

Write with apparent mastery of the topic even if you don't feel that you are mastering the topic. Rationalize your scrambled thoughts into concise focused blocks or paragraphs with neat and clear lettering. Maintain form. Track coaches tell their athletes to focus on maintaining their running form when they feel insecure and worn out in the last fifty yards of the race. The form carries them through the finish line, sometimes in first place. Present yourself as someone who is "in the know" and you will be interpreted as someone who is "in the know" by the reader. It is also important to make sure that the letters are legible. An anonymous participant who once served as a teaching assistant admitted that he used to give lower scores for less legible answers.

As mentioned earlier in the book, chaos can be dealt with by forcing it into categories. Categories are divided into subcategories, creating a grid from which to answer the question. The opposite can be true too. The student can identify or create one or more subcategories and build up to categories resulting in a grid. The grid is the basis for the student's argument.

Look at item(s) in a different context. Go to a lower or higher level. Try a more basic or more specific level. Stand back from it all or stand closer to it all, and look at it again. Change the location or the order of the pieces. Add or remove pieces. If you can't solve all of it, solve some of it. Answer individual pieces at a time and then put what you have together.

10.3 Short-answer Questions

"Ask the professor if it is okay to give outlined answers to short-answer questions," a student at the University of Illinois proposed. "You can cram a longer list of points into your answer and it saves time. Short-answer questions are often graded based on the number of points that you list. For example, someone who lists seven points might get a higher score than someone who lists five points, even though the number of points that the student is supposed to list is not specified in the question."

10.4 Multiple-choice

Advice for multiple-choice questions included the following suggestions: If there is a chart or graph, consider studying it before reading the question. Circle or underline key words as you read the questions. Translate double-negative terms into positive terms. For example, the term "not none" can be translated into the term "some." After reading the question, think of the answer in your head. Then, look for your response amongst the available answers. Look at every possible answer before answering because the key is to pick the best option, not just one that is true. Cross out the ones that are clearly wrong. Look for cues in the question and eliminate as many answer-choices as possible. Then pick an answer. Pick the one that is right instead of the one that looks right. Answers that have extreme terms like "all," "none," "always," or "never" are often wrong. Here, favor the more conservative options. Options with terms that are not absolute like "sometimes," "often," and "in some cases" are often right. Answers that are true in theory but not in fact (or vise versa) are often wrong. Avoid answers that are correct in and of themselves but not correct with the question stem. "Look for patterns," a student at Auburn University said. "Frequently instructors will put the same answer twice as a choice but word them differently. When two choices say the same thing, they cannot both be the correct choice, if only one can be chosen. The answer is often one of the two similar answer options. Also, if two choices completely contradict each other, and are all-inclusive, one of them is likely to be the correct choice. If the choice is between a graph having a mean greater than its median or less than its median and the option of them having the same mean and median is not presented, then all other choices can be ruled out as it must be one of the two. The mean must be either greater or less than the median and therefore it must be one of the two answers listed above." Be aware of grammatical construction. Wrong answers sometimes have misspelled words or bad grammar because the person who created the examination was careless in formulating alternative answers. The best answer is often the one that correctly uses the course's terminology. In some cases, it helps to work backwards. In some science courses, answers can be determined based on the units of measurement or by considering the relationship between formulas.

Another strategy is to label possible answers or components of possible answers as "true" or "false" to get closer to the actual answer. The student can replace some of the words with his own words or restate the whole question in his own words and try to answer the question. "If you can only narrow an answer down to two options," a student at Tulane University said, "pick the one that sounds best." A student at the University of South Dakota suggested studying the previous tests to be aware of patterns: "If the answers to multiple-choice questions on previous tests tend to be the ones with the longest answers, when you are stuck on a question during the test and have no idea what the answer is, you might pick the one with the longest answer." In the last instance, if there is no penalty for wrong answers, guess. It is better than leaving the question blank with no chance of receiving credit for it. "Once you have made a choice," a student at the University of Wisconsin-Eau Claire advised, "don't come back later and change your answer, unless you are absolutely sure." Accepted wisdom for multiple-choice and true-false questions is to go with your first answer. As student at the University of California at Berkeley claimed, "I have tested myself on whether or not to trust my first instinct. When I went with my first instinct, I guessed correctly one third to one half of the time. Stick with your first instinct because it goes with context and familiar sounding words." You might write a note next to the multiple-choice question to indicate your line of thinking at the time. If there is some argument about the question when the test is returned, there is proof on the page of what you were thinking at the time.

10.5 Matching Format

"Start on one side and go down the column on that side from top to bottom," a student at Eastern Illinois University suggested. "As you do so, answer those that you are absolutely sure of first. Next, do the ones that you are somewhat sure of. Then do the rest. If you choose one wrong match at the beginning, it can 'screw up' the remaining matches to be made."

10.6 Remembering Things

"If you are having trouble remembering something during the test," a student at the Massachusetts Institute of Technology advised, "think of the five senses that you experienced at the time you originally learned it. What were the sights, sounds, smell, touch, or tastes? What were your emotions and mood at the time? Why were you feeling this way? Where were you? Who was there with you? Where was the teacher standing? Where was the information on the page? What was the order? What figures or pictures were nearby? What were you thinking of at the time? What were you daydreaming about? What was the temperature? The mind works by associating memories; so any one of these can trigger a memory."

If you continue to draw a blank, just write whatever information DOES come to mind. This can trigger memory. It also gets something down on paper. The fact that something is on paper is an argument for partial credit.

10.7 Extras

The principles for extras in homework assignments are also applied in tests. "Everything that adds a grade point counts. Do all extra credit. Leave no point unturned." "Add a few obscure details that will capture the grader's attention." "Make it a memorable experience." "Aim at exciting a bored examiner. You will entertain yourself at the same time and get more points." "Briefly tie some things together and include something they won't find in anyone else's test, like information you learned from a journal." If you are arguing the professor's views, try to do so better than he does by adding information you've learned in a publication, other classes, or life experiences. "Tell Dr. X something he or she does not already know." In some cases, this does not require extra brains but a few seconds of creative thought. Sometimes, "the difference between first place and second place is one small piece of information."

10.8 Summarize

If you are running out of time, write a summary of what you would have written if you had enough time. For example, if there are thirty seconds left and you don't have time to write the last essay, summarize what you would have written by writing an outline, flow chart, box chart, table, or figure. These summary measures can provide a large amount of relevant information on paper in a short time. This is also applicable to parts of questions that are left. If you have already written the summary measure on scrap paper (for or from an earlier part of the test), add this scrap paper to the test and write the appropriate question number on it, so that it becomes part of your response to this test question. You can write, "I ran out of time!" above, below, or on the side of the summary measure.

10.9 Last but Not Least

Don't leave the examination until time is completely up. Check over the test even if you are confident of your answers. As a student at Clemson University said, "A careless mistake becomes a STUPID mistake when it is something that could have been caught if the test was simply checked over." "I caught several idiot errors I made during tests by simply going back a last time and scanning for little mistakes," a student at the University of California at Davis offered. "Several times," a student at Central Michigan University said, "I have accidentally filled in the wrong bubbles to questions that I actually knew; I caught these mistakes by going back over the test." Don't leave the test early to impress your classmates or for ego because grades are not distributed based on these criteria. In the long run, people will forget who left first but the grade is permanent. Make sure that you haven't skipped any questions or left areas blank. Rework trouble areas. Make sure the answers are in the right range and have the right units of measurement. Replace words and erase marks that could be misinterpreted. For number or word problems that are written out, make sure to distinguish the final answer from the other steps in the process. This can be done by underlining, circling, or enclosing the final answer in a box. This reduces confusion and makes things convenient for the grader. The grader will appreciate you and your efforts.

SECTION 11: AFTER TEST

11.1 Celebrate

An anonymous student said that she does not like to talk about test questions with other students immediately before or after the test because it makes her feel anxious. "Pat yourself on the back," a student at the University of California at Berkeley encouraged. "Your sincere effort is the reason to celebrate."

11.2 Check the Grading

When a test is returned, go over the grading of each question to make sure it was done correctly. Sometimes there are innocent mistakes. Issues of short cut, convenience, and strained schedules can also result in errors in the grading of assessments.

11.3 Assess the Assessment

Analyze the assessment style, wording of questions, areas of emphasis, source of the questions, type of answers that the teacher expects, and how points were distributed. This is to fine tune preparation for the next assessment. "One of the most obvious patterns that I have found is the test style of a particular professor," a student at Central Michigan University said. "Most professors have a style that they follow when they are writing a test. It helps to just be perceptive." Sometimes you learn how information should be presented.

11.4 Learn From the Results

Learn the answers to the questions that you got wrong as well as those that you got right but were not sure of at the time of the test. Some students go a step further and find where the answer is in their notes or in their textbook to reinforce the point. A student at the California Institute of Technology said, "If the material is important enough to be on an examination, the student should certainly understand it."

Consider some questions: What kind of mistakes did you make? What type of questions did you do well on or not do well on? Which of your preparation methods worked well and which ones did not? Which of your test-taking methods worked well and which ones did not?

"The old saying 'If you continue to do what you did, you'll continue to get what you got' is true," a student at the University of Michigan at Dearborn insisted. If you did not get what you wanted, learn from it. Regroup and define a new strategy based on this new information.

"Each of us are individuals," a student at Hampton University said. "Find formulas that work best for you. Then use the same formulas over and over again." "If you did well," a student at Yale University suggested, "ask what you can do to do even better. Seek your potential."

A student at the University of California at Berkeley said that "It is especially important to continue studying hard even after receiving a high grade on the first midterm. It is a common mistake to allow oneself to slack off because of an early high grade. Even if you are pulling a top score in the class, you should still work to excel on the final examination. In classes where I received A+'s, I did not aim to get the high grade; it just came because I continued studying."

SECTION 12: TIME

12.1 Evaluate Use of Time

Think of what little things are taking up too much of your time and consider eliminating or reducing them. One student at Clemson University said that he felt that going back and forth to the library was taking up too much of his time and that he could save time by studying at home. He said, "It takes a few minutes to get there, a few minutes to settle down once you're there, a few minutes to pack up when you're ready to leave, and more minutes to get back from the library. All of these sum up to quite a bit of study time. I found it more effective to cut out distractions at my desk and concentrate at home."

12.2 Use Each Day

"Work on the course a bit everyday," an anonymous student suggested. "Do something everyday on each class. At least read a page or look at a problem. Take advantage of days when you have a light homework load to look ahead." "Do some homework every single day even if you don't have class that day," a student at Embry-Riddle Aeronautical University said. "Whether it's completing an assignment, reading ahead in textbooks, or simply reviewing material, it's much easier to stay ahead when you accumulate daily points."

12.3 Take Advantage of the Extra Time in the Day

There is more time in the day than many people think. As a student at the University of Hawaii pointed out, "There are times before classes, between classes, and after classes where small goals can be accomplished. I went in early, during lunch, and after school before practice to work on my projects." Bring work with you for the "in-between" times when you will be waiting. Study a bit here and a bit there. Even if it is only one paragraph, you are one paragraph further ahead. "Never turn your mind off," a student at Clemson University insisted. "What does that mean? It means, when you're done studying, every once in a while, quiz yourself on things. If you're standing in line, waiting for the lady behind the glass shield to dish some of that stuff they call 'mashed potatoes' onto your plate, instead of just bemoaning how it will taste to the person behind you in line whom you've never met, ask yourself something about a subject from class. I don't ask myself questions I know; I try to think of the things that I had difficulty with."

12.4 Combine Tasks

"I do more than one task at once," a student at the University of Colorado at Boulder said. "I complete mindless tasks that can be done on 'autopilot' while occupying my mind with academic work. I study equations that I place on my mirror with post-it notes while I brush my teeth." "I read class notes, proofread papers or glance at flash cards during television commercials," a student at the University of Michigan at Dearborn remarked. "These things can also be done while doing other things like eating lunch, working out on a treadmill or stationary bike, doing laundry, ironing clothes, stuck in traffic, waiting in line at the bank, riding the bus, or walking across campus to the next class. I do not recommend studying while driving your car though. I did this and got in a fender bender but I did get a top score on the test!"

12.5 Switch Subjects

Instead of taking a break, simply switch to another subject. This can be a great break from the first subject and a new adventure. Then, when you get tired of the second subject, you can switch back to the first subject or another subject without taking a break. This saves time. A similar strategy is to switch tasks within the same subject. If one task is too long, do a shorter task; make use of the smallest period of time.

12.6 Establish a Regular Schedule

"It helps me to create a regular schedule," a student at Laramie County Community College said. "I set aside specific times that I will study (for example, from 3 to 5 PM and from 7 to 11 PM). The habit keeps me working through good and bad times." A student at Yale University finds that he studies well on campus. He deliberately stays on campus everyday until 8 PM to study; this daily schedule allows him to get work done.

Some people have more energy at certain times in the day. Whether you are a day person or a night person, you can pick the periods of time in the day that are best for you individually and make it regular. "I tend to go brain dead in the afternoon," a student at Indiana University of Pennsylvania admitted. "My peak hours are at night." A student at the University of Illinois at Chicago said that he works faster and wastes less time late at night.

Once you have made a decision about your regular study hours, tell your relatives and friends what these times are. If there is a long block of time that you must stay away from them for study, let them know in advance when this time will be. They will know when it is okay to approach you and when you are available to attend events. If you just say "no" to their invitations and do not notify them of when you are available, some may assume that you are never available or that you are not interested in a relationship.

A student at Central Michigan University said that during his designated study times, he disconnects the telephone to prevent calls and to prevent him from checking his email every few minutes or playing on the Internet. A student at Clemson University places an "away" message on her door when she really needs to get studying done.

12.7 Last Minute

As a student at Yale University said, "Never schedule anything for the last minute because there is no last minute."

12.8 A Bit Behind?

If you are behind in a course, do the current reading first. Go back and address the reading that you missed in your spare time, for example, on the weekend. If you do the opposite and read the chapters that you missed first, the result may be a continuous cycle of catch-up.

12.9 Little Time Left?

If you are running out of time, don't panic. Gain composure and stay calm. As a student at Mansfield University of Pennsylvania advised, "Have a PMA (Positive Mental Attitude)." Define a systematic approach. For example, first decide what needs to be covered. Next, decide which of these things you will cover in more detail, which you will cover in less detail, and which you will sacrifice. Next, order the pieces. Decide what you will do first all of the way to what you will do last. Now you have a specific plan which is a series of pieces from the first to last. Thrive on this new plan, one piece at a time.

The first step above was to define what needs to be covered. When they are behind, if it is for a test, some students rely for the most part on their lecture notes. A student at the University of Cincinnati pointed out that "Most professors prefer their own words and emphasis over those of the text." Another student, at Tulane University, said, "If you are running out of time, stick with the notes. Forget about those three, four, or five books, even the primary textbook, because they aren't going to make up the bulk of the examination." The second step was to decide what things you will cover in more detail, what you will cover in less detail, and what you will sacrifice. Some students have their instructor make this decision for them. Some instructors also have materials that already summarize the important areas. "If I don't even have enough time to review my lecture notes," a student at Carnegie Mellon University said, "I focus on those notes that will garner the largest number of points on the test." The third step mentioned above was to order the pieces. Decide what you will do first, all of the way to what you will do last. "I do the parts of my notes that I know the least well first," a student at the University of Oregon said. "Then I do the parts that I know better." The last steps listed above were to follow the plan, and thrive on it. This strategy for dealing with time that is running out is similar to the approach discussed earlier in the book for accomplishing individual goals. A goal is defined. It is broken down into small pieces. The pieces are ordered. One piece is addressed at a time.

Some students described how they get through individual pieces. As a student at Columbia University advised, "Treat each piece as if it is the only thing in the world at the time." "Imagine all that you could accomplish in one minute if you truly sought your human potential in that moment," a student at Princeton University said. "Pretend that you are just experimenting with your human potential. Then, you will start to pick up pace." "My strategy," a student at the University of Alaska at Fairbanks said, "is basically very brief and very focused studying. I try to live each moment fully, putting all of my energy and focus into the activity at hand."

Some students get through individual steps in their plan by making an agreement with themselves that they will not leave their desk, cubicle, room, or building until they have finished a particular piece of the plan. Some decide in advance to study in specific blocks of time, like half hour or one-hour blocks of time. Others pace themselves and work steadily with very short breaks between each section.

"Read selectively," a student at the University of Illinois advised. "Read with a purpose in mind." Some students use systematic short cuts for the pieces of the plan that they will cover in less detail. For example, if part of what will be covered in less detail will be certain parts of textbooks, short cuts can entail reading chapter introductions, summaries, and overviews. As a student at Western Oregon University Honors College said, "Whoever thought of printing overviews at the end of each text chapter was a saint." Closely examining the headings and titles of each section; definitions; bolded, italicized, or highlighted words; and diagrams, figures, or tables are also options. "One short cut is to 'top' and 'tale' paragraphs as you read," a student at Oxford University said. "Read the first and last one or two sentences of each paragraph, skipping the middle section of each paragraph. Most experienced writers introduce the topic at the beginning of the paragraph. At the end of the paragraph, they give the core feeling or essence of the point they are trying to make. The middle of a paragraph is essentially 'detail' or 'stats' that may not contribute, in some instances, to the core learning."

"When I fall behind in my physics classes," a student at the University of

California at Berkeley said, "what I try to do is to reconstruct the logical chain of reasoning behind the important results. So in thermal physics, for instance, when I am feeling lost, I will try to re-derive all of the important formulas and remind myself how they link together. In fact, I try to think of how I would reconstruct it at the time that I originally learn it so that everything fall into place later."

Friends: "I play catch-up by calling on friends and classmates," a student at Central Michigan University said. "Remember the directory of classmates that you established at the beginning of the academic term? This is a time to use it. You know who the competitive people are in your class. They may clear up areas of concern quickly as they are thinking of the same things. Some students have materials that summarize the important areas. You will of course return the favor at some time or perhaps you already have."

"You should have at least one 'study buddy' in every class," a student at Central Michigan University advised. This can be someone who you at minimum contact every once in a while to say a few words all of the way up to someone who you study with on a daily basis and are close friends with. Try not to make times of despair the only time that you call him or her. This should be a by-product of the relationship, not the only part of the relationship. As a student at Columbia University suggested, "Rely on your classmates for help. Group study sessions are wonderful; you re-enforce what you know and learn what you slept through."

12.10 Place It All in One Document

"On writing assignments," a student at the University of Wisconsin-Eau Claire said, "when I am in a hurry, I copy a bunch of information from different sources and paste it all into one long document. Then I read through it several times; I re-organize and remove something each time."

12.11 Use the Reference Librarian

"When you are behind," a student at the University of Virginia said, "make use of a resource that many students do not, the reference librarian. Knowing resources and how to get to them quickly is their specialty. Some people fail to realize how knowledgeable and skillful the reference librarian is; the service is free too."

12.12 Sleep Less?

Many stressed the importance of getting a good night's sleep. One student at the University of Pennsylvania said that in some cases he has no option but to get less than an ideal amount of sleep. "If you sleep on the floor of your dorm room in a sleeping bag," he remarked, "it's a lot easier to wake up after four or less hours of sleep than if you sleep in a big comfortable bed with the snooze button within reach."

12.13 Extensions

Some students ask for an extension. In some cases, zero to few points are taken off. "If you ask for an extension," a student at the University of Cincinnati said, "do so as early in the process as you can. Give the instructor a specific plan of action indicating how you will spend the time in an organized way. This increases credibility." A student at King's University College in Canada tries to avoid getting extensions on assignments because to him an extension means that other work will pile up in the meantime and he will end up in a cycle of being behind.

12.14 Dishonesty?

At the last moment, some students call in sick. One student said that some students download papers from the Internet, using links at studyworld.com/term_paper_links.htm.

SECTION 13: LACK OF INTEREST

As a student at the University of Wyoming pointed out, "We all have had those required classes that we'd just rather leave out of our whole college learning experience. There may be a class that you signed up for that looked fascinating in the class schedule, but in reality it's quite different than what you expected." Some students offered advice for dealing with lack of interest.

13.1 Facilitating Activity

Link the uninteresting material with a facilitating activity. "For me it is a bath," a student at North Carolina State University at Raleigh said. "Every night, I take a bath and then I am able to read for at least an hour or two." One anonymous student likes to talk with her boyfriend on the telephone for an hour after getting home. Then, she can study well for the rest of the night.

Sometimes the facilitating activity is another class. A student can study an interesting class for a while, switch to studying the uninteresting class, and then switch back to studying the interesting class. A similar approach is to switch tasks within the same subject. The interesting task pulls the uninteresting task across the finish line.

The facilitating activity can be a reward. As a student at the University of Washington said, "It is much easier to study hard if you know that you will receive a break or some reward before too long. I like to study hard for twenty minutes at a time with five-minute breaks between each twenty-minute interval. At every third or fourth interval, the break is for fifteen minutes." "Define in advance what the reward will be and how long it will last," a student at the University of California at Los Angeles advised. You can adjust the frequency of the reward to the difficulty of the material. Different rewards were suggested. These include exercise, listening to music, watching a television program, talking on the telephone, reading a newspaper, and watching a video. "My roommate and I used to do step aerobics or watch Aladdin after studying for an hour," a student at Central Michigan University said. "It sounds stupid, but it worked for us!" Some people read fun books. "I set up a reward system that is paced," a student at North Carolina State University at Raleigh said, "like one chapter of a favorite junk or trash novel per chapter due for a class." "I keep short books or books with short stories around my home for these exact moments," one anonymous student said. "Short books or stories are better because they aren't able to take my attention away for long, since reading them doesn't take long. Usually, I can read for just a little while and then go back to working with a refreshed mind and attitude. 'Mindless' reads such as romances, fantasy, etc. are good choices for this type of anxiety-reducing reading." "Usually I will take a shower," a student at Boston College said. "It doesn't take long and it's relaxing. I clear my head, let my mind wander, and then return to studying in a productive mindset." Some students meditate during the break. Examples of meditation include yoga or chikung. Sometimes the reward is more space on the weekend. "I make sure every night I touch some of the assignments due so that I can possibly have free time on the weekend," a student at North Carolina State University said. For some students, the reward is simply the effect that it will have on their grade point average. As a student at the University of Arizona at Tucson said, "My drive was how it would affect my overall grade point average." "I was always extremely driven to get a good grade, and keep my grade point high," a student at DePaul University remarked. "That was the chief motivating factor in dealing with classes I did not like."

Some students plan study times around scheduled social events. "I arrange to study before events that I want to attend," a student at

Southern Arkansas University said. "This conditions me into believing that studying is fun because it leads to a positive outcome every time. I actually enjoy studying this way. I can take pleasure in the social event without a guilty conscience too."

13.2 Find the Interesting Parts

"No subject is completely uninteresting," a student at Central Michigan University insisted. "Find aspects that are interesting and expand from those points."

13.3 Associate It with Things You Already Love

This is one way to make the subject yours. Drive discussion towards these interests. As a student at the University of Alaska at Fairbanks suggested, "If you like dance and you are studying romanticism, you might ask, 'How is body language related to romanticism?'"

"Talk with the professor, frankly, about your lack of interest," a student at Brigham Young University advised. "Share with him or her your educational and professional goals, and talk about a way to integrate the subject matter into your interests. He or she can lead you to specific resources that might be of more interest to you."

If the class is required to write an essay, you might ask if you can write yours on this link. "If your final project is writing a paper on some event in theatre history," a student at Brigham Young University said, "you might be able to devise an alternate final project that would require just as much work but that would fit better into your learning style or area of interest. Perhaps you could create a video presentation that chronicles the different acting styles from early America until now or write a one-act play that deals with the history of the theatre during a specific time period. Almost always, professors are impressed that you are willing to do just as much or more work on a project that would help you learn the same material, just in a way that fits you better." The rest of the class and the teacher can learn from what you find on this.

"Choose your individual way to reach the goal," a student at the University of Wyoming insisted. "Not only will this make the mundane seem more lively, but it will strengthen those neural networks in your brain that are necessary for retaining class information for an exam!"

13.4 Speak With People Who Love the Subject

In addition to the instructor, other students in the class often have personal experiences that lead them to be passionate about the subject. Ask these people why it is that they love the subject so much. "Through them," a student at Auburn University School of Pharmacy said, "I gained insight that I had never considered before. For instance, university core curriculum requires that a student take two literature courses. My major is pharmacy, and I saw absolutely no point reading literature that I didn't understand. I sought out a friend of my roommate's, an English major, and we talked about the significance of literature. Through this friend, I saw the importance of learning how to express one's thoughts through writing and how to decipher the thoughts of others through reading. Now literature isn't so bad. It is still not my favorite class but it is interesting now that I understand better its purpose." Ask the interested person if you can study with him. The person might keep you excited about the subject during the course. Since that person is passionate about the topic, he might also have additional information that is insightful.

13.5 Take It With a Friend

"To deal with lack of interest," a student at Idaho State University suggested, "take the class with a friend. You and the friend can compete for grades. Between me and my friend, whoever gets the lowest test score has to take the other person to lunch. Whoever ends up with the lowest final grade in the class has to treat the other person to dinner."

13.6 Establish Interest Through a Tutor

"There was one course that was required for my major that I was absolutely dreading," a student at Hamilton College said. "I was not interested in the subject matter and I was also not academically strong in it. The first week of classes, I decided that the only way to get through this course was to get a tutor. It was the best decision. My tutor and I met every Saturday, and went over the previous week's work. During the week, I would read the material and write down any questions that I had; my tutor would answer these questions at the end of the week, in our Saturday session. The class had a quiz every Monday on the previous week's material, so meeting my tutor on Saturday forced me to study early and consistently throughout the week. Having my tutor (someone who was not only excellent in the subject but also enjoyed it) enabled me to get into the material. I still hated it but it was much easier with my tutor helping me. So my advice for students would be to get a tutor, not only if they are failing at the end of a semester, but in the beginning. Don't be afraid to get a tutor. It shouldn't be an embarrassment. Other students and also your professor can know you are getting this extra help only if you want them to."

13.7 Help Others and Challenge Yourself

If the reason for the lack of interest is that you already know the material or are more advanced than the other students in the class, one approach is to help other students. As a student at the University of Wisconsin-Eau Claire said, "It was mostly a review for me but I still learned a lot from that class by helping other students understand the subject. I got a lot more out of that class than I thought I would." The student can also challenge herself with additional assignments and in some cases get credit or extra credit for it. "When I find myself under-challenged," a student at the University of Texas at El Paso said, "I often choose an assignment option that is contrary to my usual stance, kind of like playing the devil's advocate. Justifying something that is not known or natural makes the assignment more interesting."

13.8 Pretend

One way to get through "uninteresting" material is to pretend that you are a specialist in the field, are majoring in the subject, or are the subject itself. "I have often found history classes somewhat boring," a student at Clemson University admitted. "However, sometimes, when I would open my book, I would think of myself as a historian or archaeologist, uncovering an artifact from centuries ago." A student at the University of Wyoming said, "Find a way to make it MORE than what it seems." "Pretend that you are an extraordinarily curious person with an insatiable desire to know more about it," a student at the University of California at Los Angeles said. "Tell yourself that your brain can take on much more than this and that you feel insulted at such little information," an anonymous student suggested.

13.9 Read Out Loud

"Read it out loud," a student at the University of Florida maintained. "You hear it with your ears while you see it with your eyes. It is as if you are studying it twice at one time. This will help you to focus. It is the same technique used in emergencies. If there is a fire, you pull out a fire extinguisher and read the instructions on it out loud to help you focus despite what is going on around you." A student at the University of Oregon pretends that he is reading to a large audience to make the process more profound. A student at the University of Illinois does the opposite; he pretends that someone else is reading it to him.

13.10 Approach the Subject as Pure Learning

Responses from students included the following seven: "Treat the subject as an adventure, a discovery of a new land. It opens new horizons, and broadens one's understanding"; "Approach it as pure learning. Learn it just for the sake of improving your mind. It is the gained knowledge that is interesting. Tell yourself that it is good for you"; "Who knows, you might learn something you never thought you would. I have taken classes that I thought were going to be boring but I learned some things that I never would have picked up anywhere else. Do not let yourself fall behind just because you are not interested in the subject"; "Every piece of information you learn helps to make you a more knowledgeable and cultured person. An informed person is a great treasure"; "Subjects that seem unalike at first glance really do overlap later on. The information can come in handy and be valuable later or across a lifetime. For instance, I don't find math very exciting or interesting but I remind myself how useful it is. Math is needed for many things"; "You will never know where the knowledge from a class may help you later in life or even on the job. I had no interest in physics at the undergraduate level and I am now working in a field where this is important"; "No subject is completely useless."

13.11 It is Not Forever

"I just tell myself that I won't have to study it forever," a student at the University of Illinois at Urbana-Champaign said. "The class will end soon enough; so make the best of it."

13.12 Get it Off Your Chest

"Bitch and moan before trying to study," a student at the University of Wyoming proposed. "Once you've run out of things to whine about, you can get down to business. For me, Geology 1100 was the most boring thing in the world. I couldn't have cared a lick less for rocks. Whining everyday helped."

13.13 Make it a Top Priority

Increase the priority status of the "dull" course. Sit in the front of the class; pay more attention; make your ears and eyes larger; absorb more detail; place more emphasis; and ask more questions. Comments included the following: "You can identify more with the subject if you are an active participant in the class." "Use the boredom as an excuse to get even closer to it. Use it as an incentive to get ahead and get all of the work done early."

SECTION 14: STRESS

Methods used to deal with lack of time and lack of interest can also be used to deal with stress. Additional methods to deal with stress are discussed below.

14.1 Deep Breathing

Responses included the following: "To relax right away, close your eyes, inhale for five seconds, hold your breath for a second, and then exhale for five seconds. Do this at least three times"; "Keep telling yourself, 'I am relaxing. I am feeling better now'"; "Talk yourself into it but also imagine yourself into it. Imagine your muscles relaxing in the process"; "Imagine a quiet peaceful place"; "Have a glass of water."

14.2 Good State of Mind

Comments from students included the following: "Surround yourself with cues from positive thoughts and relaxation"; "Inventory those things that put you in a good state of mind; then create a regular routine with them. With this you will be in a good state of mind on a regular basis.... Inventory the things that put you in a bad state of mind, and slowly remove them from your schedule and environment. These things include thoughts, actions, behaviors, people, and things in one's surroundings"; "Finish studying on a good note like finding the answer to a really difficult problem"; "Every night before I go to bed, I read something for fun (not course related) for around twenty minutes and then I fall asleep in a good mood"; "Be secure in your faith"; "For spiritual reasons, I have decided to reserve a day of rest every week; on this day, I do not study my course work."

14.3 Take a Nap

"I've found that if I'm feeling stressed," a student at Carnegie Mellon University said, "a nap typically does wonders for my anxiety level. It gives me a chance to regain my composure. When I wake up I feel more prepared to attack the problem."

14.4 Find Private Time

"Find a time and place each day where you can have complete privacy and quiet time. Take time off from other people and from pressures. Short time-outs during the day can help improve efficient functioning for the rest of the day." It can be helpful to choose a structured activity for this.

14.5 Have Positive Relationships

Comments included the following seven: "Don't drift along in troublesome and stressful situations or relationships. Take action to change the situation or relationship for the better"; "If you don't get along with someone who you have to work with, identify the person's positive characteristics, and compliment the person for these positive things. You will appreciate them and they will appreciate you (in words and actions)"; "Every negative event is accompanied by a positive opportunity"; "Ask yourself if you will benefit more by doing the opposite of what your emotions tell you to do"; "If you ever get involved in a major conflict with someone, wait until the sun comes up again before you respond. Great ideas come up in the following day"; "Consider the power of indifference. This is good for you, your emotions, the situation, and other people. Sometimes people are simply trying to get a reaction from you and lose interest if they do not get one. Use confusion too. Think of the adage, 'If you can't convince them, confuse them'"; "Consult with your friends and family when you have problems"; "Establish a tight network of friendly, academic, and professional contacts."

14.6 Be Disrespected

No matter how great you are, there will be a certain percentage of people who de-value or disrespect you and your work. Consider the ten greatest leaders of our time. For each of these leaders, there are millions of people who dislike and de-value them, despite their great work! Consider the president of the country. No matter who he/she is at a particular point in time, a large percentage of society dislikes him/her. There is variation in our society and in criteria for judgment. Don't be bothered if you run into someone who quickly de-values you, and your work. Be surprised if it doesn't happen to some degree.

Those who are the best are also the worst, in the eyes of some. Some like to have statements prepared in advance like, "There is no perfect work. There will always be some limitations."

14.7 Morning on the Day Before

"If I have a big assignment due in a day," a student at Carnegie Mellon University said, "I'll get a good night's sleep, wake up early in the morning on the day before it is due, and do it in the morning instead of staying up until 3 AM the morning it is due. By doing it on the morning before the day it is due, I don't experience both fatigue and stress at the same time."

14.8 Clean Your Environment

"My room sometimes gets messy as I am swamped with work and other things to do," a student at Hamilton College admitted. "I have found that cleaning helps to reduce the anxiety of a large task or assignment because it gives me a sense of accomplishment and a reminder that I am in control of my life. After I do a little straightening, I always feel better prepared to tackle the task in front of me."

14.9 Start From Where You Are

Don't worry about previous failures. Start from where you are now and move in an upward direction. Start a new trend. Take pride in increments of improvement. Human beings adjust best to physical, emotional, and psychological changes that take place in increments.

14.10 Physical Activity

Comments included the following six: "Regular physical activity is known to reduce stress"; "It improves general health, boosting overall endurance and stamina, and helps me maintain a level of mental intensity"; "I find that exercise gives me energy for the rest of the day"; "I work out once a day no matter how busy I am; I have found that this tends to help me think clearer and to be a happier person"; "I engage in a vigorous physical exercise that is convenient and pleasurable. Sometimes it helps to get a friend to exercise with me"; "If you are too embarrassed to exercise outside or in front of other people, do it indoors. Exercise can be done anywhere and at any level. Stretching without exercise is even good for you and reduces stress." Some of the sports that students mentioned included walking, running, soccer, basketball, mountain biking, skiing, snow shoeing, aerobics, and weight lifting.

14.11 Other Activities

Other activities that reduce anxiety were mentioned. "I knit, I read, I sing, I draw, I bead," a student at Clemson University said. "So many students focus so hard on academics that they forget to expand their minds through the humanities. These avenues help me to feel more well rounded and also help me to relax and de-stress from studying and classes." Some students mentioned listening to music, watching cartoons, watching the news, and watching movies. "I watch TV or listen to music while I get dressed," a student at the University of Illinois at Urbana-Champaign remarked. "This minimizes my stress and puts me in a good mood. My favorites are Rachmaninoff and Enigma. I walk in and walk out of the examination with a smile." "On the way to a test listen to Beethoven's 5th," a student at Washington State University at Vancouver suggested. It structures the mind." Other activities that were mentioned to reduce stress include cooking, taking pictures, building collections, building models, doing volunteer work, and spending scheduled time with special people.

14.12 Diet

Diet can affect physical, emotional, and psychological well being. Think about the composition of foods and slowly incorporate a balance of health foods into your routine. As is the case with bad habits, it is hard to get out of a good habit once it is established.

"Use alcohol and other drugs wisely," a student at Idaho State University cautioned. "Be in control of it, not vice versa. Avoid the use of sleeping pills, tranquilizers, and other drugs to control stress."

"I saw many cases where students were bouncing off the walls from too much caffeine, and one girl took so much Nodoz, she was too sick to go to the examination," a student at Georgia Institute of Technology remarked. "Here is an example of what not to do," a student at the University of California at Berkeley offered. "Once for another pair of organic chemistry and physics tests, I got so nervous before the chemistry test that I didn't eat all day, took some double espressos, and bounced off the wall the entire examination day until my friends force fed me a power bar. After the examination, I crashed and had to drink a carton of apple juice before I felt up to reviewing physics."

14.13 Keep Busy

"This may sound bizarre," a student at King's University College in Canada said, "but I like to keep myself busy. I get involved in extracurricular activities to fill up my time. This is good for two reasons. First, it forces me to budget my time and thereby limits my time to procrastinate. The more things I have to do, the more things I get done. Secondly, it gives me something besides school to enjoy and gives me a release when things are not going well. This helps me to stay ahead because I have a route to vent my school frustrations. Then, when I go back to it, things aren't as bad as they first seemed."

14.14 Pretending

"An anxiety-reducing method I use is pretending I am taking a test for someone else," a student at the University of Hawaii said. "It sounds rather silly but for me it works. I pretend I'm taking a test for a close friend of mine. It reduces my anxiety and gives me a sense of control." "Approach the examination like it's any old quiz, and the grade doesn't matter," a student at the Massachusetts Institute of Technology advised. "Once you stop focusing on getting a good grade and just concentrate on writing down what you know, the information will start pouring out of you without you realizing it."

14.15 Some Stress is Good For You

"Anxiety is natural," a student at Idaho State University insisted. "Accept it. Some anxiety is good for motivation." It is when anxiety becomes too high that it becomes a problem.

14.16 Translate the Stress

"Just before an examination," a student at Trinity College in Australia said, "when I have a feeling of nervousness or panic, I consciously try to turn it into a feeling of excitement instead. I use that adrenaline in the examination to make me work faster instead of panicking blindly." "I go into examinations firing myself up like I'm going to take it down," a student at Stanford University said. "My best examinations are when my adrenaline is pumping and I am writing down answers quickly but accurately."

14.17 Run Towards the Challenge

As a student at Idaho State University said, "View life as challenges to seek, not obstacles to avoid."

14.18 Don't Compare Yourself to Others

"I find it helpful to think of learning/studying as my own personal goal/path," a student at the University of California at Los Angeles said. "If I compare myself with other students, then I become nervous and can't feel as comfortable and calm while studying."

14.19 Condition Yourself to the Conditions

Familiarize yourself with the conditions of an event before the event to increase the chance of feeling comfortable once the event takes place.

14.20 Coach Yourself

Positive visualization is one way to reduce or prevent stress. "Before any examination," a student at Brown University said, "I visualize myself walking into the test room, sitting down, and going through each question, whatever it may be, and answering it correctly." Self-coaching is an excellent way to deal with stress. "This is similar to what a coach does before a big game," a student at Clemson University said. "Using college football as an example, all teams have a locker room ritual that they perform before a game. Therefore, when teams leave a locker room from a coach like Tommy or Bobby Bowden, they are ready to play. Also, at most big schools, the team will run out to the fight song and do so with much pomp and fanfare. Some examples are Clemson University with running down the hill, Osceola at Florida State University, and the Sooner Schooner at Oklahoma. What is being said here is that everyone needs a pre-game pep rally. Since you are your own coach, you have to provide it. I always found that a good fast song works. You should choose the song carefully, and it should speak to your interests and personality. I use 'Eye of the Tiger' but for someone at or from Alabama or Auburn, 'Sweet Home Alabama' might be more fitting. This anxiety is purely psychological and can be beat just as any athlete beats it before a big game."

A student at the University of Texas at Austin said that "When I get stressed about a class or an examination, I remind myself that I have worried in the past about not being successful yet I've always pulled through with a good grade."

"Cut-off negative sentences before they are finished," an anonymous student said. "In fact, cut them off before they start." "Take your mind off of self-defeating thoughts," a student at Idaho State University advised. "For example, before a test begins, I picture my summary notes. I rehearse key concepts and terms, instead of worrying."

"Encourage yourself through difficult times by using entertaining but meaningful adages like, 'I may be an unsung hero today...but not tomorrow!'" a student at the University of Cincinnati said. "You might also consider the use of labels that are less intense than the circumstance. Less intense labels can translate into less intense emotions."

"The trick is that you have to relax to study effectively," a student at Brigham Young University insisted. "If all that's going through your head is, 'I'm never going to learn all this in time!', then you probably won't. When you're calm and focused, you can pull off better grades with less study time, and less stress."

"A certain part is an arrogance or belief in myself," a student at Loyola University of Chicago said. "I just tell myself that 'everyone is cooking with water' and that I am actually better at this particular subject because I have prepared and researched it." A student at Southern Arkansas University said that he looks at himself in the mirror everyday, smiles, and tells himself that he is good. Before each type of activity, he tells himself that he is good at that particular activity. He convinces himself before he gets there.

It's only a test. Responses included the following seven: "It is only one test"; "Your life will not end if you don't get an A+"; "You will still go on breathing and eventually it will be forgotten"; "The trouble with anxiety is that it blows everything out of proportion; small things seem like life or death matters and make or break moments. Simply put things in context"; "I also have begun to realize that if I do bad on one examination, ten years from now I am not going to even remember what classes I took a certain semester much less what I got on a test in some science class. Since I have begun to relax when test taking and when preparing for tests, I have seen a significant increase in my test scores"; "By letting go of the goal of the grade, one releases the anxiety"; "Know that grades are not everything and that the more important thing is what you learn and how you can apply it in real life situations." As a student at Loyola University of Chicago said, "If I do not know tiny little details, this is not a failure but human." There is always more detail about the topic that can be learned.

"Remind yourself that school isn't that bad," an anonymous student proposed. "There are millions of people who would rather be learning than doing what they are doing or being where they are right now."

Will power was a theme. Comments included the following four: "Will power is my anxiety-reducing mechanism. I simply decide not to be stressed and I'm not. I remind myself that worrying isn't going to help anything and that I can put my energy to better use by studying"; "Keep telling yourself that your best is good enough. Believe in your own ability"; "My approach is utmost confidence. Walk into the examination with a smirk on your face and a sharpened pencil (and wit) in hand. I truly believe that 90% of any challenge is mental"; "I approach everything with a can-do attitude, and when I am faced with examinations, I focus intently on the task at hand. All other possible distractions fade away and all the ongoing absorbing that I have done thus far floods forward to my mind so that I may use the knowledge for the examinations. I also feel that no one is any smarter than me, so why shouldn't I do well? Examinations are not designed to fail everyone but to recognize those who have prepared. Also, I feel that it will be okay if the material is too difficult for me to master it within the time constraints. I can go back and review it later. The goal is to learn, not to gets A+'s; as long as I have that perspective, then most times, A+'s will come from the learning process. Learning for the sake of learning causes no anxiety."

Just Do It. Comments included the following ten responses: "Still can't? Then just do it!"; "Choke it down and memorize it anyway"; "Simply put your head down and work"; "Learn to just buckle down and get it down"; "Sometimes you just have to jump through the hoops"; "Grin and bear it"; "As you work, it will become interesting to you"; "After you know the information, it starts to grow on you. If it doesn't, at least you'll know that information"; "What pushes you in your academic career is yourself. Yes it sounds corny but it is often your mind that is the main stimulus towards success. You have to just put yourself in that chair and study the material no matter how boring it is because that is the only way you can achieve your goals. Who said the road to success is paved anyway? The result is nevertheless welcoming"; "Force yourself to do all of the work."

SECTION 15: FINANCE

15.1 General Advice

"If you are having problems with money," a student at Hampton University suggested, "re-evaluate how you are using it. Make a list of what is being bought and the reasons. Remove or decrease those things that have a lower priority. Then stick to your new list."

"I eat cheaply," a student at Green River Community College said. "Top Ramen and fruits." Some foods, like fruits, vegetables, and bran are not only good for health but can be cheaper than some popular foods. Money can be saved by cooking or eating in the cafeteria instead of going to fast food or other restaurants. Some students suggested eating and living with relatives. Other money-saving ideas included: borrowing inter-library and regional library books and CD's instead of buying them; borrowing or bargaining for books, CD's, or other materials from friends and teachers or at web sites like booksfree.com; selling books that the student no longer needs at sites like swapbooks.com, online book auctions, bookstore buy-back programs around campus, at the public library, or at a book fair; photocopying specific sections of readings instead of buying the entire reading; downloading free software programs and books from the Internet from sites like download.com, zdnet.com, netlibrary.com/, or bookspot.com/ask/ebooks.htm; doing research on the Internet; avoiding alcohol or drugs; reducing entertainment spending; cutting back on what was previously interpreted as "necessary" spending; washing clothes by hand; spending less on clothes; and using cheaper transportation. "Students should remember that they are students; they do not have to impress anyone," a student at North Carolina State University said. "All too often, students worry that they have to have the latest CD, newest clothes, or a top of the line car. These things aren't necessary and people do not expect them out of you. There is plenty of time after graduation to get all your wants and dreams."

15.2 Money From Others

For college-level students, one suggestion was to determine how much money will be needed per unit of time before approaching relatives or friends for money. Determine in advance when and how you will pay the person back, if appropriate. This clarity is good for both parties. It is organized, shows that the student is serious, and allows the relative or friend to make good decisions for his/her own finances.

Other responses were the following: "Speak frequently with your financial aid advisor to keep up with any changes"; "Those who ask for more, get more"; "There are people who are willing to give you money for your hard work as a student, through scholarships, but you have to be willing to look for it and then do what is necessary to apply. It is worth it!"

15.3 Jobs

A student at Stanford University held that "The best jobs are those which offer experience in the student's area of study." "A part-time job puts all the theory into application," a student at the University of St. Thomas at Houston said. "Both of the jobs I had while in school were in the communications field and therefore added to my education rather than taking away from it," an anonymous student said. "They worked synergistically with my education." A graphic design student at Portland State University worked part-time as a freelance designer while attending school. A student at North Carolina State University said that "Part-time jobs help you to learn time management skills and to broaden your network of people. I worked at the student center ten hours a week scooping ice cream, and four hours a week babysitting. I learned to organize and prioritize my assignments and extra activities. I learned how to utilize every hour of my day. I read during down time at my jobs and during lunch. I wrote papers on napkins between customers at the ice cream shop and then typed them while babysitting (with the permission and use of the family's home computer)." "For the first year and a half of my graduate years," an anonymous student remarked, "I worked a job that was commission-only (advertising sales) and had an understanding with my employer that school was my priority. I was given a lot of flexibility to complete my job as I needed to, in order to make money to cover my expenses." "The key was finding a job or jobs that allowed me to be a student," a student at the University of St. Thomas at Houston said. "I could study when there were no calls coming in. My bosses knew that I was a student and didn't mind letting me bring my homework with me. Most of the time, my bosses were very interested in what I was studying as well; so we could have conversations." "I hold a job at our Student Recreation Center," a student at Eastern Illinois University said. "On this job, I can use my time to do my homework, as well as make money. There are jobs like this at every school. The programs are more than happy to give these jobs to A+ students and even happier to do so if you qualify for work-study."

SECTION 16: AFTER COURSE

16.1 General Advice

After the course, celebrate, assess, correct, and learn. Find out your final grade early so that if the grade needs to be changed, it can be done before the grade is sent to the administration. Once the grade gets to the administration, it may be more difficult or impossible to change. Some schools have change of grade procedures that may be pursued.

"At the end of the semester," a student at Indiana University of Pennsylvania suggested, "say goodbye to your teacher, how much you enjoyed the class, and that you are glad you took it. Don't burn your bridges. Stay positive all of the way through."

16.2 Storage

"At the end of the course," a student at the University of South Dakota remarked, "I recommend putting all of your papers, notes, flash cards, examinations, tests, assignments, and syllabus into one place like in a binder, manila envelope, or accordion file (whatever works for you). Label it with the course title, code, professor's name, and when you took it. In the future, it may be needed for a grade dispute, another course in the subject, a wish to 're-educate' yourself on the topic, or an interest in helping a friend."

16.3 Keep Going

Put the semester behind you. Make a new assessment of the coming classes and instructors. Start earlier than needed. Begin as if you are the underdog for the next academic term.

16.4 Congratulation

If you received an A+, congratulations. If you earned an A+ but did not receive one, congratulations. "Always evaluate yourself first," a student at Mansfield University of Pennsylvania advised, "and then take other's judgments into account." As a student at Indiana University of Pennsylvania said, "In either case, knowing that the grade does not make the person is critical." "For me," an anonymous student said, "it is the academic journey, not the result, that is worthwhile." A student at the University of Illinois at Urbana-Champaign said that "If you have a blast doing your homeworks/projects and still do bad, stick to your guns...be persistent. You will be a fantastic professional, one of those few that excels because of their enthusiasm and love for the field." A student at the University of Kentucky at Lexington said that "School gives us practice developing some QUALITIES that ARE valuable in the real world. They are persistence, self-discipline, enrichment, broader perceptions, personal satisfaction, knowledge, leadership, learning how to learn, learning how to find and use information, ability to think independently, and ability to work under pressure. These things we take with us wherever we go!"

SECTION 17: SUGGESTIONS FOR EDUCATORS

Some students offered suggestions for educators. It was agreed in advance that these responses would be completely anonymous. The following twenty-two points summarize their comments.

17.1 Learn from History

Before the academic term begins, an educator can identify areas for improvement in the course by studying the history (and results) of the course from the perspective of administrators, faculty, students, people who touch their lives, and people whose lives they touch. In the past, how did each person contribute in positive and negative ways; passively or actively; and consciously or subconsciously? Did each person find his or her potential in the process? Were short cuts taken in some places? Were some things done or not done for the sake of convenience? What role did good intentions play and what were the results? Were some gaps filled with speculations or assumptions about structure, circumstance, or people? Each component and step in the process can be studied for pros, cons, and potential for change. Areas for improvement can be found, and the educator can define a specific plan of action. The plan might include the people, services, materials, and schedules that will be needed to achieve the targeted improvement(s). The next step is to act upon it before the term begins.

17.2 What is Important to You?

People respond to things that are important to them. These important things drive their lives. Each of us lives in a different world and has a different combination of obstacles to face. The question, "What is important to you?" goes to the heart of matters. This question can be asked in different ways, angles, levels, and frequencies. It is one way to address differences in background, circumstance, experience, culture, gender, and age.

Things that are important for and to the student can be incorporated into the plan of action, lesson, titles, acknowledgements, climate and way in which the educator interacts with the student. A lesson or part of a lesson can be created from these items or expand upon them.

Related questions that can receive the same treatment include the following: "What are your needs?", "What works for you?", and "What am I missing here?" All of us are missing something about other people and their needs.

17.3 Be Organized

An educator can create a syllabus, study guide, lecture notes, and/or outlines for class. Useful information includes title, subject, day, date, instructor, purpose, objectives, corresponding chapters in the course text, optional reading, and relevant comments for individual classes or deadlines. Additional information can include: rules; procedures; format; grade distribution; contact information of instructors and/or their secretaries; office hours; office locations; drop off and pick up places; and locations on campus, off campus or on the Internet of related and relevant information or tools.

Some students are impressed when the instructor brings necessary and optional materials to class instead of expecting students to find a way to produce or borrow them. An instructor can make arrangements with the administration or other institutions in advance for the students to have materials for designated classes. An instructor can also apply for a small grant in advance for this purpose.

If photocopied material is distributed, make sure that distinguishing characteristics are not missing. Graphs and legends commonly lose elements in the photocopy process. One student said that if it doesn't cost much more, instructors should make color copies of key graphs, figures, or pictures (or use a computer to generate them). This shows the instructor's extra dedication and can help to make the learning process exciting for the student.

17.4 Sound and Letter Size

One student said that if the students in the last row in the class cannot hear, the teacher is not speaking loud enough. One strategy is for the instructor to gear the volume of his voice towards the last row of the class throughout the lecture. At the beginning of class, the teacher can ask the students in the last row if they can hear clearly. One student had an instructor who spoke loud in class like a drill sergeant. The student loved it because he could hear every word clearly and it kept him awake. There are students in different parts of the room, for different reasons, who need the volume.

Similar advice was given for letter size. If the smallest letter on the board cannot be seen by the students in the last row, the letters are not large enough. Letters that seem large to the teacher at the board may still be unrecognizable in the back row or from certain angles in the class. The idea is to make letters larger than it seems necessary. The teacher can write a word on the board and then go to the back row before class begins to see how well she can see the word from there.

17.5 Enthusiasm

Express love and fascination for the topic through facial expressions and body language. Ninety percent of communication is non-verbal. An instructor can smile. A smile expresses happiness and creates happiness for each party. If the instructor is fascinated, students will become fascinated by association. Explain what it is that is exciting about the topic, and why this topic is important. Before each subsection, explain how the student will benefit by having the knowledge or skills of this subsection. Try to make it a thrilling process of discovery for students who dislike the topic the most. If you inspire the most resistant of students, the rest come easy. One student said that the best type of teaching inspires a love for the subject, not just an understanding of it. Some educators speak monotonically and give the impression that they themselves have little interest in the topic; as a result, some students lose interest or never establish it.

17.6 Don't Read Lectures

Try to give the lecture, instead of reading the lecture. When an instructor reads a lecture, the impression is that the instructor does not know the material well himself. One strategy is for the instructor to pick words or phrases that cue him into each section to be presented. The instructor can create a wild story (that he keeps to himself and that includes these cued words). He can think of this story as he gives the lecture. With this, he will be able to give the lecture smoothly without having to look down at a paper or book and read it. This can be applied to whole lectures or parts of lectures.

17.7 Clarity

One of the most common complaints from students is lack of verbal clarity. Simple and well-pronounced words are key. Since students love clarity, don't be afraid to overdo it. Clarity also reduces the chance of misinterpretation. Often there are many different legitimate ways to interpret the subtlest of differences. The teacher can orient the students by clarifying the day, date, title, and current location in the lecture series at the beginning of each lecture. She can clarify what things were for the previous lecture and what things are for the next lecture, at the beginning or end of each lecture. Inform the students of reading and writing assignments in advance. Define what something is but also make a few points about what it is not. This crystallizes the edges. Similar advice is to describe what the student is expected to learn but also take a brief moment to point out the areas that the student is not expected to learn at this stage in the training. Since more than thirty percent of the brain is engineered for the interpretation of visual images, a teacher can help by deliberately choosing simple clear images for the board that can be used to explain more than one aspect of the topic. One student suggested repetition: summarize what will be taught, teach, and then summarize what was taught.

17.8 Complete Notes

One thing that is important to students is a complete set of notes at the end of the lecture. It is frustrating to a student to leave the class with a fraction of what he wanted on paper. An instructor can help by engineering this agenda into the class. For example, when a teacher is presenting slides, he can plan time into the lecture for students to write all of the words on the slides, ask if everyone has finished before moving on, use more concise slides, provide photocopies, or make the information available on a web site.

17.9 Order

Some teachers zigzag back and forth between topics in lecture. By the end of the lecture, the student's notes are a mess. It is useful to present one topic at a time with clear breaks between each and a predefined order. The notes will then flow in a way that will make sense to the student when he reviews them at a later point in time.

17.10 Objectiveness

Make a sincere effort to be objective in the presentation and evaluation of information. Consider both (or more) sides. Some students complained that some teachers only present one view, pressure students to accept the teacher's personal opinion, or restrict consideration of other views in class and on graded assignments.

17.11 Assumptions, Biases, Culture, and Tradition

Describe common assumptions, biases, cultures, and traditions in the field (and why they exist). Spoken or unspoken, every field has these. The student needs this information to know the difference between objective and subjective elements of the field, to communicate in an acceptable way with peers in the field, and to complete certain steps in challenges (like homework problem sets). Simple examples include the assumption that the average man weighs 70 kilograms and the tradition of presenting power in joules per second. There are other logical ways of presenting the information but some are not accepted in the field of study. Some teachers forget to include this information because it has become automatic for them.

17.12 Examples

Give specific and complete examples with different scenarios. Examples provide many forms of useful information in a short period of time. Humans of all sizes learn effectively through example. When a mother teaches a baby what a table is, she points to a table and says "table." The baby receives verbal information from the mother's voice, visual information from the movement of the mother's lips and from the view of the table, and information about the table's texture by touching it. Information is received from many different angles. This is how adults learn too, through example. The same is true for analogies. Finding complete examples and analogies can be difficult for the teacher but is well worth the effort. It increases the standard of understanding and students love them. If for some reason time does not permit, the teacher can provide examples and analogies on paper for the students to take home and study.

17.13 Challenges

Teach and then test. Some of the students asserted that some teachers test before teaching. As a result, the student has no basis from which to answer the questions. Other ideas were the following: spend a disproportionate amount of time teaching verses testing; teach for understanding instead of for testing; give tests that are fair representations of what is taught in the class. Some instructors teach one thing but test on something else. Another suggestion was to de-emphasize memorization and focus on the structure of knowledge, the general rules of the domain, and strategies for the problem-solving process. After teaching with many clear examples, give assignments that have the student constructing or transforming something. Give assignments with a good gradient of questions. An example would be an assignment with a few easy warm-up questions, many medium-difficulty questions, and one or two very challenging ones. With a good gradient of questions, everyone gets something out of it. Each student can step on the ladder and move up. The questions might be ordered according to this gradient. Each student can begin their experience with the confidence that comes with getting the first few ones right. This encourages the students to continue; it also reduces the stress and procrastination that can accompany the beginning of a challenge. Gradients can be used for assignments and examinations.

17.14 Amount of Work

One rule of thumb for the amount of homework to assign is to assume that the students have five other classes requiring equal amounts of time. This accommodates not only the other classes but also the student's need to participate in activities outside of the class for balance and to build credentials for graduate school or post-collegiate jobs.

One student said that his instructor assigned so much required reading that most of the students rarely completed it; as a result, they seldom had something intelligent to contribute in class. If a very large amount needs to be covered, one strategy is to divide the class into groups, assign each group a different part, and have each group present or discuss their part. The benefits are that the material gets covered, the students maintain interest, and the in-class discussion is of higher quality.

17.15 Clearly Define Goals, Expectations, and Requirements

One student said that his instructor put the students into small groups without defining the goal. Each student had his own idea of the goal and nothing got accomplished. The instructor needs to be as specific as possible. A student was given general instructions, worked hard, and then found that the teacher was looking for something else. Much of the student's hard work was done in vain.

17.16 Get The Student There

If a student just doesn't fit into the teacher's system, the teacher can help the student achieve the goal in another way. A participant of the survey has a brother with dyslexia. Letters of some words appear backwards or upside-down. As a result, he could not take the written examination like other students. So his teacher read his test questions to him out loud. The student proved verbally that he knew the answers well despite the reading difficulties associated with dyslexia. There is often more than one way to achieve and to demonstrate excellence.

17.17 Legitimate Problems

One student said that life is happening to the student at the same time as the course, and only in Utopia will the two never conflict. Leave room for the possibility of legitimate problems when they do occur and work with the student. Sometimes things happen that are beyond the student's control; the student only survives if the teacher has faith.

17.18 Derogatory Words

One student asked for clarification of a test question that she felt was poorly worded. She had never been angrier in her life than when the teacher's response was to ask her if she knew how to read. She said that students pay to be in class but not to be humiliated or talked down to. Derogatory comments, particularly from someone who students look up to, can be painful and have long-lasting effects.

17.19 Respect is a Two-way Street

Students usually have fewer credentials and are younger than the teacher. However, humans of all ages and backgrounds respond best to relationships in which both parties are treated with respect.

17.20 Order of Scrutiny

First present the positive things. Explain how and why it is that these things are positive. Then present those things that need to be improved or changed. Describe how and why these changes will make a difference.

For a long written project, like a dissertation, consider reserving specific types of scrutiny for specific stages of the project. For example, in the first stage, an advisor might limit scrutiny to the direction of the project. In the next stage, limit scrutiny to components of the outline. Further stages of scrutiny may include: certain types of detail; sections or chapters; terminology; documentation style; and in the end, spelling and grammar.

17.21 Written Corrections

If you are correcting a draft, avoid using the color red. In Western society, red is often associated with things that are negative, dangerous, or stressful. The teacher might consider using pencil. As mentioned earlier in the book, gray is restful. Blues and greens are calm and cool. Greens are often linked with things that are positive and safe.

The teacher might write corrections in list form, on a separate piece of paper, instead of directly on the student's draft. This sends a signal that the student's draft is valuable and respected. It reiterates the idea that respect is a two-way street

17.22 Availability

Finally, many students want time in the faculty members' or administrators' schedules. In some cases, a staff member allocates responsibilities to persons below or around him but is not himself visible or available.

SECTION 18: CONCLUSION

The goal of this project was to identify some beliefs, thoughts, strategies, and actions of some A+ students (beyond genetics, sociology, and economics). What do they think that others might not think? What actions do they take that others might not take?

I learned that there are many criteria, definitions, perceptions, and allocations of A+. There are also differences in original goal. Some students set the goal of earning an A+ or a similar mark. For others, the A+ grade is simply a positive side effect.

There were other suggestions in the book that stood out for me. These included the following:

(A) Before the Academic Term:

- "Start when it feels uncomfortably early. This is the signal that you are starting at the right time."

- Take a moment to clarify your priorities and goals well in advance.

- At each step, think in terms of statistics. What will give you the greatest statistical advantage? What is the smartest thing for you to do at this moment, not five minutes ago?

- Recognize that competition starts before the scheduled event or deadline. There is competition in the activities that lead up to the scheduled event, during the event, and in activities that lead from the event.

- The functional deadline is usually before the official deadline.

- If you do it on time or late...it's late. If you do it early...it's on time.

- Doing things early is a skill. First start by doing one thing early. After seeing the positive results, you will be encouraged to do another thing early. Soon doing things early will become a habit that you just have to do. "As is the case with bad habits, it is hard to get out of a good habit once it is created."

- Leave little to chance. Do it or part of it when you don't have to do it, so that when things go wrong, it is already done.

- At least 30% of factors may be unpredictable. So incorporate time and resource buffers.

- Accomplish a goal by dividing it into smaller, more manageable pieces, ordering the pieces, and attaching a deadline to each piece towards an early false deadline. Complete one piece at a time.

- Use a daily planner, To Do lists, and organizers.

- Arrange one's environment in a way that facilitates the planned activity.

- Set a regular schedule of study, sleep, and diet.

- Choose a major, course, or a course of research that is true to your heart. Passion for the subject will increase the chance of a great performance.

- Consider alternative classes and services that exist but are not publicized.

- Courses, assessments, and instructors tend to exhibit the same patterns over time. Before signing up for a course, acquire some information about the historical patterns of the course, the course's assessments, and the course's instructors (although this information may be in rough form).

- Find out and think in detail about the criteria for the distribution of grades.

- Make a distinction between the objective and subjective components of the class. Establish a plan that recognizes this distinction.

- Once you have signed up for a course, collect more information and materials before the term begins. Begin a rapport with the instructor early. Discuss definitions or goals and how they need to be achieved. "Professors are impressed with students who show effort, intellectual curiosity, and commitment that is earnest, particularly if it is earlier than required." "Remember, most professors WANT their students to do well."

- Consider the benefits of beginning the reading before the term begins.

- Take a shorthand class during the summer (or other holiday period).

- Know that you can do anything if you set your mind to it. Coach yourself and visualize success before each event.

(B) Beginning the Academic Term:

- Start the academic term off strong. Do it now because this is when time is available. Give the draft to the instructor now so that you will get it back on time. Treat the first two weeks of the term in the same way that many students treat the last two weeks of the term.

(C) Before Class:

- Do the reading and homework for the lecture the day before, instead of after the lecture.

- Read in an organized way: Decide what you will read and your reading objectives. Preview the reading by looking at the front and back cover, preface, titles, subtitles, introduction, and conclusion. This is to identify the reading's basic categories. Predict the contents of each of these categories before you begin the reading. Read once quickly for general concepts and to determine which parts are important. Read a second time with emphasis and curious questions in the important areas. Alternatively, read once with curious questions; make predictions about what comes next throughout this one reading.

- Consider the natural senses. People who are site-oriented might find it useful to use colored pens, post-its, highlighters, written words, typed words, underline, pictures, images, diagrams, flow charts, mind maps, or figures. Individuals who are hearing-oriented can find it useful to listen to themselves, other students, or the instructors in person. They can also speak out loud, listen on audiotape, or attach a tune to the information to be learned. Those who are movement-oriented might express themselves with gestures; they can focus on the facial and physical gestures of other people. Some need to have their fingers moving with a utensil or on a keyboard. The same can be true of people who are touch-oriented; they often like to have their hands involved in constructing something. Students who are taste-oriented might find it useful to have candy, gum, or other food in their mouths. They can associate what they are learning with food or the process of preparing food. Those who are smell-oriented associate what they are learning with an aroma, perfume, or fragrance. Students can develop senses that are weak and make use of all of them. Further, the student can note what he is thinking, doing, and feeling at the time that he is learning something to increase retention.

- Writing Notes: Outline form can be used for both pre-lecture notes and lecture notes. It offers the flexibility of writing as much or as little as the student wishes and results in a clear organization of ideas on paper.

(D) Class:

- Arrive early for each class with appropriate materials. Sit in the front of the class to rid distractions, increase focus, and identify subtleties. Build relationships with students in the front of the class. Consider the possibility of adjusting to each teacher's style.

- Participate earnestly and actively in class. Be an active seeker of knowledge; predict what will be said and see if you are right. Ask yourself and others questions, use imagination, and think of how what is taught can be applied in real life. Stay in class until the end of the lecture to be there for important announcements, reviews, and opportunities to ask follow-up questions.

(E) After Class:

- Correct and/or rewrite the lecture notes soon after class on the same day.

- Review: Each time that you review your notes during the term, consider rewriting them to more condensed forms so that you have a tight manageable size of notes to review just before the test.

- Office Hours: Attend office hours to acquire more information; probe further for areas of importance; clear up issues; ensure that you remain in the right direction; stand out from others; further demonstrate who you are, your sincerity, your extra effort, your knowledge, and to attend to the subjective parts of the course. When you have questions, consider asking several different sources to increase the chance of acquiring a complete and correct answer, to learn how to do things in more than one way, and to reinforce the information.

- Homework: Start homework on the same day that it is assigned. Give yourself instructions and acknowledgements. Be systematic. Take every assignment seriously. Target the right question. Identify the intent of the assignment. Review previous publications on the topic. Don't limit yourself to definite answers. Be creative. Think across lines. Relate the topic to everyday life or to industry. Contact gurus in the field and find out what is taking place on the topic's cutting edge. Cite sources when it is not required to increase credibility. Handle chaos by forcing it into categories and subcategories. Alternatively, pick the closest subcategory and build-up to larger categories to establish a useable grid. Another way to deal with chaos is to create an outline, and further outlines, at lower or higher levels, for trouble spots that remain. Consider a different context. Confusion can be forced into the categories who, what, when, where, how, and why. Find your way to answers by questioning yourself, making use of the units of measurement, and using trial and error. As you learn, develop a step-by-step method for each type of problem. Look at your work through the eyes and concerns of the teacher. Show all of your work to accumulate partial credit. As you study, learn what needs to be learned now, instead of later. Understand as much as possible to reduce how much you will have to memorize. Study old tests and assignments. Practice to make perfect. Make use of simple summary measures like charts, mind maps, tables, acronyms, and acrostics to learn and review. Look for associations amongst words and patterns in numbers. Make the process entertaining by playing games or attaching a tune.

- Writing Assignments: Start right off the bat with an exciting title and perhaps a quotation. Use extra formal categories in the paper, including front matter and end matter. Choose a topic that you are curious or passionate about. Learn about the topic's subcategories. Consider combining these subcategories to create a thesis statement. Consider three or four possible arguments, and go for the one with the greatest support. Some students create an outline and proceed from there. Others write a draft in its natural sequence and allow an outline to emerge on its own from this first draft. For detail, the student can use both traditional and state-of-the-art search methods in school libraries and on the Internet. Search methods can include those used by journalists. Consider incorporating primary sources and primary research, as well as secondary sources and secondary research. Pace yourself and set a certain number of pages or sections to accomplish in each session. Explain one idea at a time. Describe what something is but also take a moment to depict what it is not. Include succinct examples and analogies. Describe the best and the worst-case scenarios. Refrain from repeating words and phrases. Remove unnecessary words. Consider describing circumstances and characters in action to make the reading more exciting. Use active metaphors. Include color illustrations, pictures, and accompanying legends. Reserve some of the spicy things that students would normally place in the body of the essay for the concluding section of the paper. Overextend the concluding section of the paper. In the bibliography, include works cited as well as relevant works that were not cited. Check grammar and spelling by computer but also by hand. Ask yourself questions about the quality of your work. Have others who you trust read it. Take advantage of free draft reviews by instructors. Use quality materials for the final product to complement the contents. Store each stage of work.

- Dissertations: Choose a topic that you are passionate about. To do this, consider unresolved curiosities from previous years of study on the subject or related subjects. You might consider a topic that branches off of work that a favorite faculty member is already doing. Ask simple but critical questions about the do-ability of the research topic, available tools, resources, time, and other people you will have to work with. Carefully investigate the habits of potential thesis advisors and potential members of your thesis committee. Make sure they have an interest in your topic, do not have established beliefs or biases against your argument, and will be available. Clarify expectation with yourself and authority figures at each stage. Choose a model that is conducive to your research and writing style. Do not begin research until you are personally convinced that the series of steps makes logical sense to you. Choose a model but accept variation from it, and speak with your own voice. Document and date empirical data but also what you perceive to be your own scrambled thoughts. Set a tentative schedule and deadline for each part. Present both sides of the argument and honestly include the limitations of your work. Value both positive and negative results. Recognize that a thesis does not have to solve a problem; it can instead explore and discuss its complexities in ways that others have not. Consider signing-up for a peer-editing group. Ask your experts questions before they ask you the same questions at a later point in the sequence. Acquire information from senior students in your department who have recently gone through what you are about to go through. Learn, practice, and possibly negotiate the conditions of your thesis defense before it takes place.

- Arts: Master the fundamentals of your field. Rehearse elements of the performance in isolation, and together. Rehearse related forms. Rehearse mentally. Tune-in to the immediate environment. Remain loose. Deliberately look for little things that you may not have detected before and study their details. Continually refine the work. Push it to the professional level or higher. Consider conceptual, formal, theoretical, and experimental boundaries, and go beyond them. Consider practicing the art or the piece until it feels instinctual. Exchange information with others. Immerse yourself in the history and culture of the topic or piece. Consider using pleasant landmarks. Draw from personal experience. "Do not perceive others as scrutinizing you and your every move." Perhaps you are the one scrutinizing them and their moves. "They are the ones to be apprehensive, if this is to be the case." Believe yourself. "Be open-minded to but not stuck on outcomes."

(F) Preparing for Tests:

- Prepare for tests through early repetition, practice, consolidation, and condensation of notes during the term. Start the final review one to four weeks before the tests. Do not rely on cramming. Get a good night's sleep and have a good meal before the test.

(G) Test:

- Get to the test early. Give yourself instructions throughout the test. Use a systematic approach. Scan the test. Estimate the time available to answer each question. Read each question carefully. One word can make a difference. Do easy questions, medium-difficulty questions, difficult questions, and then those that you could not complete. Interpret components of essay questions in terms of the categories who, what, when, where, how, and why. Write a brief outline on draft paper before beginning. Use clear and concise language. Write with apparent mastery and maintain form. Force chaos into categories and categories into subcategories. For short-answer questions, consider presenting points in outline form and including many points in the limited space. For multiple-choice questions, underline and circle key words in the question stem. Translate double-negative terms into positive ones. After reading the question, think of the answer in your head. Then, look for your response amongst the available answers. Look at every possible answer before answering. Avoid answers that have extreme terms, that are true in theory but not in fact, that are correct in and of themselves but not correct with the question stem, and that use poor grammar or spelling. Look for answers that correctly use the course's terminology. Consider working backwards, using the units of measurement, labeling parts of answers as "true" or "false," and restating phrases in your own words. Eliminate as many answer choices as possible and then pick an answer. If you are not sure, go with your first choice. For matching format, match the pairs that you are sure of first. To recall information during the test, think of the five senses that you experienced at the time you originally learned it. Be creative. Aim to excite a bored examiner. Tell Dr. X something that he does not already know. Make connections from personal experiences and what you have learned in other classes. Summarize what you do not have time to finish with a flow chart, box chart, diagram, table, or figure. Stay in the test room to the end and double-check answers even if you are confident about them.

(H) After the Test:

- After the test, celebrate your effort. Double check grading, assess the assessment, learn from the results, and define new strategies for yourself.

(I) Time:

- Re-evaluate your use of time. Reduce or remove those things that are taking up too much of your time. Make use of extra moments in each day. Make better use of resources that you already have. Consider combining tasks or switching between subjects without a break. Re-define and use a regular schedule. If you are behind, do the current reading first. If you are running out of time, decide which pieces you will cover in more detail, which pieces you will cover in less detail, and which pieces you will sacrifice. Then, order the pieces and complete one piece at a time.

(J) Dealing with Lack of Interest:

- Consider a facilitating activity. Find interesting parts and expand from there. Associate what you are learning with things that you love. Interview and work with people who are passionate about the topic. Consider taking the class with a friend, establishing interest through a tutor, helping others, arguing an opposing view, or addressing new aspects of the topic. Other options are to read the material out loud, engage in the art of pretending, make the course a higher priority in your life, and learn for the sake of gaining knowledge and becoming a more cultured person.

(K) Dealing with Stress:

- You can relax quickly by using deep breathing exercises. Talk and imagine yourself into a relaxed state. Don't worry about previous failures. Start from where you are now and move in an upward direction. Inventory things that put you in a good state of mind and incorporate them into your daily life. Inventory things that put you in a bad state of mind, and remove them from your schedule and environment. Consider taking a nap, finding private time, having positive relationships, waiting until the sun comes up again before responding to a bad interaction with someone, cleaning your environment, engaging in physical activity, and maintaining a good sleep pattern as well as a good diet. Familiarize yourself with and practice the conditions of the event in advance. Run towards challenges, not away from them. Translate stress into positive energy for the task at hand. Articulate your frustrations to "get them off your chest," so to speak; then, get down to work. The opposite is true too. Consider choosing terminology that is less intense than the situation seems to warrant; less intense terminology and labels might translate into less intense emotions, particularly over the long run. Consider the possibility that you "may be an unsung hero today...but not tomorrow." Coach yourself with pep songs, entertaining adages, and re-assuring words that are meaningful to you. Run your own race; don't compare yourself to others. When it comes down to it, if needed, just do it!

(L) Finance:

- Re-evaluate how you use money. Determine what is taking too much money and reduce or remove it. Consider eating cheaper, depending on relatives or friends, using equipment for free at school, downloading free programs, borrowing or photocopying needed sections instead of buying, selling books and other materials that are not being used, and buying less expensive types of materials. Stay in contact with the financial aid officer. Consider jobs that both fit your area of interest and allow school to be a top priority.

(M) After the Course:

- Celebrate, assess, correct, and learn. If you need to change a grade, do so before the grades are turned into the administration. Label, date, and store your materials. Put the semester behind you. Make a new assessment of the classes and instructors for the next term. Start earlier than needed, beginning as if you are the underdog for the next academic term.

(N) Suggestions for Educators:

- Educators can study the history and recognize things are important to each party. Identify and incorporate issues that are important to the student but unimportant to the teacher. Consider the impact of each step of the plan on the receiving end. Consider the usefulness of a syllabus, study guide, and/or class outlines. Make sure that resources work and are compatible before directing students to use them. Try to give a lecture instead of reading it. Direct the intensity of sound and letter size on the board to the last row of the class. Teach with enthusiasm. Design the lecture to energize the most resistant of students. Inspire understanding but also love for the subject. Speak clearly. Present one idea at a time, in an ordered sequence, so that the student's notes will flow in a way that will make sense to the student when he reviews his notes at a later point in time. Engineer the limited class time so that the student has a complete set of notes at the end. Put forth a sincere effort to be objective in the presentation and scrutiny of information. Be aware of the extent of your own biases or dogmatic views and don't force them on the student. Include many complete analogies and examples in the process of teaching. Teach before testing the students. Be clear about expectations, goals, and requirements for assignments and tests. Give challenges with gradients, so that everyone gets something out of it, builds confidence, and moves in an upward direction. Recognize that excellence can be demonstrated in more than one way. Avoid potentially derogatory-sounding words or statements. Articulate the positive aspects of the student's work before articulating the negative aspects of his work. For corrections of written work, avoid using the color red. Pencil is an option; gray is restful. Blue and green are also options. They are thought to be calm colors. Green is associated with things that are positive and safe. Consider writing corrections in list form on a separate piece of paper instead of directly on the student's draft. Lastly, make yourself available to students and let the students know when these times are.

Author's Reflection

The Power of When: When something is done can define the difference between a high score and a low score; great performance and poor performance; a great experience and a bad experience. If the student starts before or at the beginning of the academic term, she can experience the thrill of knowing that she is ahead of the rest of the world, enjoy the material, and take pleasure in the protection from deficits in people, the process, and the system. If she starts on time or late, the thrill of "early" is not there, there is stress, fewer available resources, lower quality resources, a lower interest on the part of others to help, less protection from inequities in the system or process, and a higher chance of failure. Those who begin earlier than the system requires often find a pattern of success.

The Power of Landmarks: Many of the students in the survey use landmarks. One example is the student who acquires applications for awards, postgraduate training, and jobs years in advance and uses the items on these applications as landmarks to be accomplished by certain times towards graduation. A second example is a priority or large goal that is broken down into smaller pieces. The smaller pieces become landmarks that are addressed one at a time. One student at Stanford University uses thirty percent as a landmark for the amount of each class's reading to be completed before the academic term begins. A student at Yale University uses the two-week point at the beginning of an academic term as a landmark to be two chapters ahead in each class. A student at Stanford University reads the homework assignment "plus at least 'one' additional thing." An anonymous student acquires at least two pieces of information from every major paragraph that he reads. A person at Louisiana State University sets a specific landmark, one to four weeks before an examination begins for the commencement of his final review for the examination(s). Clarified criteria for the distribution of grades are landmarks. Agreements between the student and instructor on the definition of definitions are landmarks. The headings, subheadings, bold and italicized words, and introductions and conclusions that are previewed before reading takes place are forms of landmarks. Previous works, components of an outline for an essay, elements of the units of measurement, the categories in a grid, and mnemonics are landmarks. The student's experiences on the five senses are used as landmarks to recall what was learned on an earlier day. Some artists use guidelines. Some musicians use landmarks in the score and some stage performers use them in the auditorium. Lawyers use statutes and judgments of previous court cases as landmarks. Physicians use bony structures in the body as landmarks to locate other structures in the body that can be more difficult to find like arteries, veins, and nerves. Landmarks can help people to assimilate, consolidate, retain, and recall information or facilitate performance.

Sorting Kinds and Levels of Importance: Students are overwhelmed with information. Many of the students in the survey pool deal with this by sorting kinds and levels of importance. One strategy is the following: Find out what you have; force it into traditional or non-tradition categories of kinds and levels of importance; and distribute your limited resources according to these categories. This can take place several times in a day. Examples include priority lists, To Do lists, the sorting of information gathered for assignments, and the sorting of information that will be covered on a test.

The Power of Questions: Many students transcend barriers by asking questions. These include questions about the historical pattern; the content of courses; teachers; the criteria for judgment; the frequency and value of events; definitions; the purpose and intent of assignments; expectations; biases; levels of importance; pitfalls; and limitations. Questions are effective tools for teachers too. The teacher can look beyond numbers, ask questions about things that are important to students, and find ways to incorporate this into the educational experience.

Convenience: Most people like convenience. Therefore one way to predict the future action of an individual (student, teacher, or administrator) is to consider things that are convenient to or for that person. In many cases, your predictions will be right.

Thank-you

I would like to thank my family members. I would also like to thank the 300 A+ students who contributed their words, thoughts, and beliefs to this book.

Appendix A: Survey Questions.

1) What is the definition of an A+ (or an equivalent mark)?
2) What is the distinction between an A+ (or an equivalent mark) and an A (or an equivalent mark)?
3) Specifically how does a student earn an A+ (or an equivalent mark)?
4) How does a student consistently earn A+'s (or equivalent marks)?
5) Describe common mistakes made by students in attempting this goal.
6) Describe uncommon mistakes made by students in attempting this goal.
7) Give an example of a universal formula.
8) Give an example of a subject-specific formula.
9) Give an example of an approach that is effective in your particular area of study.

Describe:
10) An approach that is not a formula.
11) A psychological strategy.
12) A memory technique.
13) A method to reduce anxiety.
14) A specific test-taking strategy.
15) How to deal with a particular examination format.
16) A note taking strategy (for lecture or for homework).
17) How to absorb lecture material without taking notes.
18) A reading strategy.
19) Action(s) to take before, during or after a lecture.
20) Action(s) to take before, during or after an examination.
21) Action(s) to take before, during or after a course.
22) How you handled an assignment from beginning to end.
23) How you handled a course from beginning to end.
24) How you deal with multiple examinations scheduled together.
25) Short cuts to take when you are in a "jam."
26) Strategies to catch-up when you are behind.
27) How to stay ahead.
28) Specific communications to make with faculty and/or tutors.

29) How do you deal with lack of interest in a subject matter?
30) How do you deal with time restraints?
31) How do you deal with budget restraints?
32) How do you deal with other restraints?
33) What patterns do you recognize that others do not?
34) What do you do that others do not?
35) Do you have a specific philosophy about academia/academics?
36) How do you deal with differences in interpretation/perception/expectation between student and faculty member?
37) Describe strategy for a thesis/dissertation.
38) Any suggestions to/for faculty or administrators? [Answers to this question will be kept anonymous]
39) Discuss any additional issues that should be included in this book.

Appendix B: Online Resources for Searching Newspapers, Magazines, Journals, Summary Guides, and Books (Suggested by Some Students).

http://www is the prefix for the references below.
However, http: is the prefix for those that begin with //.

(1) http://www.libraryspot.com/ask,/askfulltext.htm
(2) http://www.libraryspot.com/journals.htm
(3) http://jake.openly.com/
(4) http://irservices.library.unt.edu/
(5) http://www.publist.com/
(6) http://infomine.ucr.edu/reference/
(7) http://www.waikato.ac.nz/library/resources/ejournal_sci.shtml
(8) http://www.freemedicaljournals.com/
(9) http://www.lub.lu.se/lub/services/ejournals.html
(10) http://www.usg.edu/galileo/internet/electronic/elecjour.html
(11) http://ejournal.coalliance.org//
(12) http://ejournal.coalliance.org/info/other.html
(13) http://www.libs.uga.edu/science/fullalph.html
(14) http://highwire.stanford.edu/lists/freeart.dtl
(15) http://pppp.net/links/news/
(16) http://pinkmonkey.com
(17) http://www.netlibrary.com/
(18) http://dewey.chs.chico.k12.ca.us/news-ss.html

Appendix C: Online Resources for Dictionaries, Thesauri, Encyclopedias, Quotations, Grammar, and Documentation Style (Suggested by Some Students).

Dictionaries and Thesauri
    (1) http://www.dictionary.com/
    (2) http://www.onelook.com/index.html
    (3) http://www.refdesk.com/
    (4) http://www.library.unr.edu/depts/reference/webref/diction.html
    (5) http://www.library.fullerton.edu/ReadyRef/dictionaries.htm
    (6) http://www.thesaurus.com

Quotations
    (1) http://www.libraryspot.com/quotations.htm
    (2) http://www.concordance.com
    (3) http://www.refdesk.com/
    (4) http://www.Quoteland.com

Encyclopedias
    (1) http://www.libraryspot.com/features/encyclopedia.htm
    (2) http://www.d.umn.edu/lib/reference/dbt.html
    (3) http://www.refdesk.com/myency.html
    (4) http://www.biography.com
    (5) http://www.bartleby.com/

Acronyms
- (1) http://www.libraryspot.com/acronyms.htm
- (2) http://www.acronymfinder.com/
- (3) http://infomine.ucr.edu/reference/
- (4) http://www.ucc.ie/info/net/acronyms/acro.html

Grammar
- (1) http://www.ccc.commnet.edu/grammar/
- (2) http://andromeda.rutgers.edu/~jlynch/Writing/
- (3) http://www.wsu.edu/~brians/errors/errors.html

Documentation Style
- (1) http://www.library.unt.edu/genref/quickref/manuals.htm
- (2) http://www.library.umaine.edu/virtualref/citations.htm
- (3) http://www.wooster.edu/psychology/apa-crib.html
- (4) http://andromeda.rutgers.edu/~jlynch/Writing/
- (5) http://infomine.ucr.edu/cgi- http://infomine.ucr.edu/reference/
- (6) http://www.bedfordstmartins.com/online/citex.html

Appendix D: Online Resources for Primary Sources (Suggested by Some Students).

---

(1) http://njnie.dl.stevens-tech.edu/primary_sources.html
(2) http://njnie.dl.stevens-tech.edu/realtimedatasites.html
(3) http://www.peoplefind.com/frames/freeresources/dataindex.htm
(4) http://www-libraries.colorado.edu/ps/gov/us/federal.htm
(5) http://www.vitalrec.com/
(6) http://www.libraryspot.com/biographies/
(7) http://www.biography.com
(8) http://www.libraryspot.com/speeches.htm
(9) http://www.libraryspot.com/ask/publicrecords.htm
(10) http://www.bookspot.com/features/poetryfeature.htm
(11) http://www.geohive.com/
(12) http://www.museumspot.com/
(13) http://www.econdata.net/
(14) http://factfinder.census.gov
(15) http://www.ipl.org/div/pf/govdoc.html
(16) http://www.d.umn.edu./lib/collections/govdocs/census2000.html
(17) http://gwis2.circ.gwu.edu/%7Egprice/crs.htm
(18) http://www.fedstats.gov/
(19) http://govinfo.kerr.orst.edu/
(20) http://www.access.gpo.gov/su_docs/
(21) http://www.census.gov/prod/www/statistical-abstract-us.html
(22) http://www.odci.gov/cia/publications/factbook/index.html
(23) http://www.bartleby.com/
(24) http://www.bartleby.com/108/
(25) http://www.library.miami.edu/netguides/socopin.html
(26) http://www.indo.com/distance/
(27) http://www.ed.gov/free/
(28) http://www.thegateway.org/
(29) http://www.census.gov/ipc/www/idbnew.html
(30) http://amillionlives.com/
(31) http://www.biblio.tu-bs.de/acwww25u/wbi_en/

Appendix E: Resources for Simple Primary Research Ideas (Suggested by Some Students).

(1) Web Sites:
   http://www.LibrarySpot.com/features/scienceprojects.htm
   http://www.researchpaper.com/
   http://whyfiles.org/
(2) Book Authors: Janice Vancleave, Julia Cothron, Judith Bazler, Mary Blaisdell, Marilyn Lutzker, C. Isenberg, and Leland Graham.

Appendix F: Online Sources for Images and Maps (Suggested by Some Students).

(1) http://www.libraryspot.com/features/thousandwords.htm
(2) http://www.libraryspot.com/features/mapitoutfeature.htm
(3) http://www.graphicmaps.com/aatlas/world.htm
(4) http://www.freestockphotos.com
(5) http://www.freefoto.com/
(6) http://www.ditto.com/
(7) http://www.picsearch.com/

Appendix G: Journalists' Tools (Suggested by Some Students).

(1) http://reporter.umd.edu
(2) http://www.ryerson.ca/~dtudor/megasources.htm

Appendix H: List of Survey Participants.

Sarah Addison	University of Greenwich, England
Salma Akbar	University of Illinois, Chicago
Steve Alcauskas	Boston College
Ayan Ali	Cambridge University, England
Jessica Allen	Valdosta State University
LoriAnderson	University of Nevada, Reno
Konstantin V. Anikeev	Massachusetts Institute of Technology
Anonymous Student	Anonymous School
Anonymous Student	Columbia University
Anonymous Student	Rutgers University
Anonymous Student	Southern Arkansas University
Anonymous Student	University of California, Berkeley
Anonymous Student	University of California, Santa Cruz
Anonymous Student	University of Florida
Anonymous Student	University of Maine
Anonymous Student	University of Minnesota, Duluth
Anonymous Student	University of Nevada, Reno
Anonymous Student	University of Oregon
Anonymous Student	Yale University
Anonymous Student	Augsburg College
Julie Babush	University of Illinois, Urbana-Champaign
Christy Badgwell	University of Texas, Austin
Todd S. Baginski	University of Cincinnati
Zaynab A. Bakir	University of Texas, El Paso
Kevin Ball	Brigham Young University
Debjyoti Banerjee	Anonymous School
Kathryn Banks	Cambridge University, England
Dennis Barrington	North Carolina State University, Raleigh
Daniel Bearman	University of Florida
Sally A. Beitia	Idaho State University
Sidra Berman	Tufts University and Robert H. Smith School of Business
Amanda Besemer	Northampton Community College and Emory University
Sanyukta Sharad Bhide	University of Virginia
Nathan Paul Biles	University of North Carolina, Charlotte
Jennifer Bobier	Anonymous School
Pathompong Bodhiprasiddhinand	Oxford University, England
Dale R. Boling	Baldwin-Wallace College and Ohio University
Alex Bolinger	Idaho State University, Pocatello
Bradford L. Boyce	University of California, Berkeley
Lily Bradley	University of California, Berkeley
Michael Bradshaw	North Carolina State University
Kathryn Bransford	Indiana University of Pennsylvania
Ben Brazil	University of North Carolina, Chapel Hill
Ariana Brechtel	University of California, Berkeley
Jason M. Brown	Harvard University
Daniel Browne	Green River Community College
Robert Bryll	Wright State University
Andres Buenfil	University of Florida

Denise A. Campbell	University of South Dakota
Douglas L. Campbell	Boston College
Jenny Capps	University of Wyoming
Andres Castano	University of Illinois, Urbana-Champaign
Sara Chamberlin	University of Wisconsin-Eau Claire
Rodrigo Cerón	Brunel University, England
Ahsan S. Chaudhri	University of Michigan
Bin Thomas Chen	Mississippi State University
Elaine Chen	Brown University
Gloria Chiang	Princeton University
David Christie	Anonymous School
Suzanne Christopher	Anonymous School
Kay Claussen	Anonymous School
Benjamin S. Cluff	University of Illinois and Utah State University
Web Coates	Wharton School at the University of Pennsylvania
Brittney Cooper	Howard University
Travis J. Cossairt	University of Michigan
David Cowden	Georgia Institute of Technology
Jennifer Cowden	Georgia Institute of Technology
Mark Cramer	University of Illinois and Harper Community College
Lauren Cuozzo	Hamilton College
Ron Davidson	Michigan Technological University
Donald James Davis	Anonymous School
Peter C. Davis	Idaho State University
Chris DeVries	King's University College, Canada
Shelley Dietrick	Western Oregon University Honors College
Pam Dixon	Hamilton College
Simeon Dimitrov	George Washington University
Sally Dowlatshahi	University of Illinois, Chicago
Nikki Draper	Brigham Young University
Kerry Drozdowicz	University of Connecticut
Eric Dubrowski	University of Illinois, Chicago
Jeremie J. Dufault	University of Pennsylvania
Kenneth D. Dunne	University Maryland, College Park
Kyle S. Early	Tulane University
Jason Eden	Anonymous School
Erin N. Eisenberg	University of Pennsylvania
Joy Ekpo	Langston University
Regina M. Elkins	Eastern Illinois University
Lincoln Ellis	University of Pennsylvania
Ilan Elson-Schwab	University of California, Berkeley
Deanna Evans	Anonymous School
Morgan Eshelman	University of Wyoming
Yi-Fan (Eddie) Fang	Arizona State University
Carly Farrell	Louisiana State University
Holly Fernandez	University of Pennsylvania
Lisa Fink	Central Michigan University
Nicholas Fitzkee	Carnegie Mellon University
Gabriel P. Floud	University of Wyoming
Michelle Flowers	Brigham Young University

Rose Forest	University of California, Berkeley
Susan Foster Fox	Texas Agricultural and Mechanical University-Commerce
Taneka Francis	Columbia University
Lee Frantz	University of Nebraska, Lincoln
David Frerichs	University of Pennsylvania
Jeanne Fromer	Harvard Law School
Maribeth Gainard	University of Pennsylvania
Lori D. Galloway	University of Texas, Austin
Ernest Antonio Galvez	Anonymous School
Balakrishnan Ganeshan	Anonymous School
Erica Garcia	University of Saint Thomas, Houston
Stephen M. Garcia	Princeton University
Laura Germine	University of California, Berkeley
Georgios Ginis	Stanford University
Lynford Lawrence Goddard	Stanford University
Shalea Ann Gonsalves	Brigham Young University
Richard Goodale	University of Maine
David Gordon	Anonymous School
Kristi Elaine Govella	University of Washington
Jessica Grabiner	University of South Carolina
Shelley T. Graham	Brigham Young University
Robert Gray	University of Vermont
Suzette E. Grebe	Brigham Young University
Michael Griffin	Anonymous School
Rosarii Griffin	Oxford University, England
Kathryn Grimm	University of Wisconsin-Eau Claire
Jodi Gureasko	Carnegie Mellon University
Steve Hainsworth	Cambridge University, England
Tom Haire	Clemson University
Philip E. Hamer	Clemson University
Jameil E. Hamilton	Hampton University
Troels Hansen	University of Copenhagen, Denmark
Elizabeth Hardaway	Hamilton College
Frederick R. Harrington	Michigan State University
Courtney Harris	Hampton University
Heather Hartland	University of Central Florida
Alicia Hayden	Louisiana State University
Kelly Hayward	Arizona State University
Alice Henriques	University of California, Berkeley
Julie Hertl	University of Washington
Shannon Higgins	Central Michigan University
Anna Hillers	Loyola University of Chicago
John Eric Howell II	Tulane University
Zhihang Hu	University of Tulsa
Peter Yijian Huang	University of Minnesota
Shirley H. Huang	University of Texas, Austin
Tony Hui	Hong Kong Polytechnic University, China
Hung Edward	University of Maryland
Joseph A. Hunt	Anonymous School
Megan Hurley	North Carolina State University
David Jermaine Johns	Columbia University

Alex Johnson	University of Wisconsin-Eau Claire
Peter Kalocsai	University of Southern California
Noppadon Kamolvilassatian	University of Texas at Austin
Hilli Katzir	University of California, Los Angeles
Diana Keen	University of California, Davis
James Houston Kelly	North Carolina State University
Raja Kidambi	University of Houston
Nathan Boyd Kitchen	Brigham Young University
Stephanie M. Kladakis	Harvard University
Erica Knievel	University of Illinois, Urbana-Champaign
Lindsay Korey	University of Miami
Stephen Kosik	Fenn College of Engineering at Cleveland State University
Vicky J. Krantz	Central Michigan University
Miriam Krause	Indiana University of Pennsylvania
Stas Kriventsov	Pennsylvania State University
Daniel Kunkle	Rochester Institute of Technology
Chia-Hao La	Massachusetts Institute of Technology
Cliff A. LaCour	Louisiana State University
Jennifer Lambert	Hamilton College
Amanda L. Langley	Louisiana State University
Salette Latas	Eastern New Mexico University, Portales
Joseph LaViola	Brown University
Sandy Leaton-Gray	Cambridge University, England
Ian W. Lebby	University of California, Berkeley
Eun-Hui Lee	Anonymous School
Wilfred K. C. Lee	University of Hawaii
Laura Leslie	University of Wyoming
Charles Liao	University of California, Berkeley
Gretchen Liechty	Indiana University Bloomington, School of Music
Amy Ling	University of California, Berkeley
George Liothake	Rutgers University
Doug Liou	University of California, Berkeley
Lisa Litherland	University of Illinois, Urbana-Champaign
Janos Tobias Locsei	Trinity College, Australia
Anna C. Long	Seattle University
Ivan Lui	University of Hawaii
Ian Lynam	Portland State University, Oregon
Amit Mahadik	Utah State University
Karla Marquez	University of Texas, El Paso
Amy Matteson	University of Michigan
Earl Matthews	Bowie State University
Robert-Emmanuel Mayssat	French Electronic and Information School, France, and University of Maryland, College Park
Kimberlie McCowan	University of Colorado, Boulder
Delia McGarry	University of Virginia
Tereyna McLeod	Kansas State University
Meggan M. Means	Central Michigan University
Sofya Medvedev	George Mason University
Catherine Mendenhall	Yale University
Susan Mentges	Andrews University

Leslie A. Merriman	University of Alaska, Fairbanks
Christian Michelson	Georgia Institute of Technology
Elizabeth Milnarik	University of Illinois, Urbana-Champaign
Vlatko Milosevski	University of Florida
Jasmine Mistry	University of Houston, Clearlake
Sarah Mongeau	Clemson University
Roberto Monteiro	University of Porto, Portugal
Garrett Moritz	Harvard University
Tara Motroni	University of Albany
Christopher R. Mudge	Louisiana State University Agricultural and Mechanical College
Kwame Musonda	University of Arizona, Tucson
Evelyn K. Myrth	Hamilton College
M. Nafis	California State Polytechnic University, Pomona
Abra Carroll Nardo	Indiana University, School of Education
Judy W. Nduati	Nairobi Evangelical Graduate School of Theology, Kenya
Lisa Nguyen	Anonymous School
Adam Nolte	Massachusetts Institute of Technology
Josh Norman	Kumamoto Graduate School, Japan
Sarah M. Nunley	Louisiana State University
Ryan Odom	Anonymous School
Dana Parker	University of Kentucky, Lexington
Nihar K. Patel	Louisiana State University Agricultural and Mechanical College
Alison Payne	Boston University
Tonya Pazzaglia	Mansfield University of Pennsylvania
Jenny Rae Pearson	University of Wisconsin-Eau Claire
JoAnna Perry	Hampton University
John D. Perry	Clemson University
Tomer Persico	University of Haifa, Israel
Stephen Petrus	Clemson University
Stephen Pohl,	Central Michigan University
William O. Poteat	North Carolina State
Betsy A. Powell	Idaho State University
Brandon Prasnicki	Minnesota State University, Mankato
Lisa D. Puckett	Central Michigan University
Raghu P. Raman	University of Florida, Gainesville
Sara Rawlings	Mansfield University
Lauren Rhone	DePaul University, Chicago
Barbara Rickman	Auburn University
Paul Riseborough	Oxford University, England
Rhett S. Robinson	Clemson University
Michael Rock	University of Colorado, Boulder
Paul E. Roundy	Utah State University
Sara Russell	Hamilton College
Jun Saito	University of Hokkaido, Japan
Michael Salitrynski	Mansfield University of Pennsylvania
Stephanie Sandeen	University of Michigan, Dearborn
Terrance Savitsky	Cornell University
Mindy Saxton	Idaho State University

Anne E. Schenck	Emory University
Krystyn Schmerbeck	Hamilton College
Ryan Searles	University of Wisconsin-Madison and Illinois Institute of Technology
Reuben J. Sebego	University of Botswana, Botswana
Emily Sensenbach	Hamilton College
Sarmad Shaikh	Harvard University
Ahmed Shams	Alexandria University, Egypt, and University of Southwestern Louisiana
Derek Shannon	North Dakota University
Mischa Shayovitz	University of Cincinnati
Lorraine Sherry	University of Colorado, Denver
Trinity Shertz	Indiana University of Pennsylvania
Sue Showalter	Indiana University of Pennsylvania
Lilia Shtarkman	University of California, Berkeley
Lindsey Shultz	Carnegie Mellon University
Guilan Siassi	University of California, Berkeley
Jimmy Simons	Clemson University
Neil Simonsen	City College of New York
Jennifer Sims	Hampton University
Christine M. Siverd	Carnegie Mellon University
Clay Smith	University of Nevada, Reno
Rachel Smith	University of California, Berkeley
Ranvir Solanki	Anonymous School
Marin Soljacic	Princeton University and Massachusetts Institute of Technology
Xubin Song	Virginia Polytechnic Institute and State University
Tara Spitzer	Hobart and William Smith College
Michael Z. Spivey	Princeton University
Zach Steele	North Carolina State University
Nedra Stennis	Anonymous School
Katie E. Stevens	Louisiana State University
David Strasburg	University of California, Berkeley
Thomas Strohmayer	Embry-Riddle Aeronautical University
Xiao-Ping Susan Su	University of California, Berkeley
Ricardo Suber	Hampton University
Katherine M. Taake	Eastern Illinois University
Simeon Tabakov	Anonymous School
Wayne R. Taitt	Harvard University
Soo Chuen Tan	Anonymous School
Sean Tang	Stevens Institute of Technology
Carrie Taratuta	Central Michigan University
Lazina Tarin	Central Michigan University
Mihail Temelkov	Anonymous School
Michelle Thurmond	University of Florida
Tara Tiedemann	University of Wisconsin-Eau Claire
Patricia A. Till	Central Michigan University
Raymond To	University of California, Berkeley
Carla Toebe	Washington State University
Hao T. Ton	Colorado School of Mines
Melissa Townsend	Indiana University of Pennsylvania
Jeremy Tsiopanas	Virginia Polytechnic Institute and State University

David Vanderbeek	Ricks College/BYU-Idaho
Pamela Vartabedian	University of California, Berkeley
Georgia Veith	Elmhurst College
Michael Wall	University of California, Los Angeles
Ashley Christine Weaver	Northern Arizona University
Cris Weller	University of Texas, El Paso
Russell West	Laramie County Community College
Delonna White	Anonymous School
Paul S. White	Washington State University, Vancouver
Jeffrey R. Wiggin	Anonymous School
Laura Wiggins	Auburn University School of Pharmacy
Sam L. Wilcke	California Institute of Technology and Reed College
Melissa A. Wilhelm	Central Michigan University
Benjamin Williams	Baylor University
James A. Wilson	Princeton University
Meagan Wilson	Drake University
Jonathan W. Wittwer	Brigham Young University
Steve Wooden	University of Illinois, Urbana-Champaign
Roger Woodsmall	Anonymous School
Courtney Liana Wooten	Stanford University
M. Kendra Wu	University of Michigan
Xu Nanjing Yingying	University of Technology, China
Meredith Young	Brigham Young University
Julia Zamorska	University of California, Berkeley, and University College Utrecht, Poland
Danlu Zhang	University of Michigan
Dmitry Zhukov	Binghamton University
Brian John Zuelke	University of Wyoming

Index

A

Accomplishing Goals 20
Acronyms 63
Acrostics 63
Across Lines 83
Act it Out 100
After Class 59
After Course 177
After Test 143
Amount to Write in Class 52
Arts 119
Attend Class 45
Appendix A: Survey Questions 205
Appendix B: Searching Publications 206
Appendix C: Writing Tools 206
Appendix D: Primary Sources 207
Appendix E: Research Ideas 208
Appendix F: Images and Maps 208
Appendix G: Journalists' Tools 208
Appendix H: Survey Participants 209
Availability 188

B

Bed 96
Before Class 31
Before Lecture Begins 47
Before Test 125
Before the Term 5
Binders 24
Box Charts 62
Bridges 65

C

Challenge 167
Chaos to Categories 88
Choosing Classes 9
Cite Sources 76

Class 45
Coach Yourself 168
Color 53
Common Sequence 65
Conclusion 189
Condition Yourself 168
Confidence 66
Context 88
Continuous Refinement 121
Corrections 188
Correcting Notes 60
Create Your Style 122
Creativity 82
Crunching the Rest 62
Cutting Edge 69

D

Demonstrate 72
Derogatory Words 187
Diagrams 62
Disrespected 163
Diet 165

E

Educators 179
End of Lecture 58
Environment 32
Examples 66
Exchange Information 121
Extras 140

F

Facilitating Activity 153
Familiar Groupings 64
Finance 5 173

First Things First 5
Five Senses 57
Flow Charts 62
Four-times Approach 94

G

Give Him What He Wants? 100
Goal 4
Good State of Mind 161
Group 93

H

Hard Part Verses Easy Part 83
Highlighting 39
History and Culture 121
Housing 6

I

Identify Details 121
Images 62 99 208
Instructions (Give Yourself) 75
Illustrations 62
Intent of Assignment 75
Instinct 121
Introduction 1

J

Jobs 174

L

Lack of Interest 153
Landmarks 122
Learn It Now 85
Lecture-note Format 51

M

Major 8
Master the Fundamentals 119
Mentally Rehearse 120
Merging the Notes 60

Moving onto Campus 18
Mind Maps 62
Mneumonics 98
Money From Others 174
Monitor Progress 102
Morning on the Day Before 163
Morning of the Examination 129

N

Nap 162
Note Cards 61 97
Number Association 64

O

Objective and Subjective 72
Objects 65
Office Hours 67
One on One 69
Other Actions Before Class 42
Other Material Before Class 40
Outcomes 123
Overlap 66

P

Personal Experience 122
Physical Activity 164
Play Games 100
Positive Relationships 162
Post-It Notes 98
Practice Makes Perfect 90
Preparing for Classes 13
Presentations 101
Pretending 167
Previous Publication 76
Previous Two Lessons 95
Previous Week 95
Priority 19 160
Probing 69
Problems 187
Projects 12
Pros and Cons 87

Q

Quality 69
Question Yourself 86

R

Read 31
Read Out Loud 159
Rehearse Related Forms 119
Relate to Everyday Life 77
Relate to Industry 77
Remain Loose 120
Remembering Things 139
Re-organizing Notes 61
Repetition 94
Repetition with Shrinkage 94
Respect is a Two-way Street 187
Respect Teacher 49
Review 125
Reverse Your Perception 123
Rewriting Notes 59
Right Question 75

S

Same Day 96
Same Numbers 99
Say it Outloud 99
Search the Internet 78
Serious About Everything 84
Seven-times Approach 95
Shorthand 54
Show Your Work 93
Sleep 128
Slides 56
Songs 66
Specificity 68
Speed 55
Start From Where You Are 164
Start Today 75
Step-by-Step Method 89
State of Mind 161
Storage 83 177
Stress 161
Study the Teacher 56

T

Tables 62
Taking Notes in Class 50
Test 131
Test Format 61
Time 145
To Do Lists 22
Through the Teacher's Eyes 82
Trial and Error 86
Type It 97

U

Underlining 39
Understand It 85
Units of Measurement 87

W

What is an A+? 1
What You Will Do Next 89
When to Attend 67
Word Association 64
Work 12
Write It 96
Writing Assignments 103
Written Assignments 31
Written Corrections 188

Y

You Can Do It 25

Order Form

Give the gift of **Survey of 300 A+ Students** to your friends, colleagues, students or family.

1 book = $14.90
2-4 books = 20% off = $11.92/book
5-99 books = 40% off = $8.94 per book
Bookstores (1-99 books) = 40% off = $8.94/book
100-499 books = $8.00/book
500 or more books = $7.30/book

Shipping and handling to locations in the USA: $3.90 for one book and $1.90 for each additional book (for up to 10 books). If 11-50 books, shipping is $1.00/book. If more than 50 books, shipping is $0.50/book.

Shipping and handling to locations outside of the USA: $5/book for 1 book, $4/book for 2-4 books, and $3/book for 5 or books.

If you are interested in having Kenneth Green speak or give a seminar to your company, association, school, or organization, contact the address below for more information.

_____ copies of the (8.5 x 11 inches) print version of book.

_____ copies of the PDF version (per computer to use it).

Please charge my ____ Visa ____ Master Card ____ American Express
or ____ Check or Money Order.

Make checks payable and return to: Crème de la Crème Press, 2342 Shattuck Ave., No. 101, Berkeley, CA. 94704-1517, USA.
[http://www.freewebs.com/honors   Tel/Fax: 206-600-6082]

Total Amount = $_____

Name _____

Organization _____

Address _____

City/State/Zip _____

Phone _____ Email _____

Card# _____ Exp. Date _____

Signature _____

Order Form

Give the gift of **Survey of 300 A+ Students** to your friends, colleagues, students or family.

1 book = $14.90
2-4 books = 20% off = $11.92/book
5-99 books = 40% off = $8.94 per book
Bookstores (1-99 books) = 40% off = $8.94/book
100-499 books = $8.00/book
500 or more books = $7.30/book

Shipping and handling to locations in the USA: $3.90 for one book and $1.90 for each additional book (for up to 10 books). If 11-50 books, shipping is $1.00/book. If more than 50 books, shipping is $0.50/book.

Shipping and handling to locations outside of the USA: $5/book for 1 book, $4/book for 2-4 books, and $3/book for 5 or books.

If you are interested in having Kenneth Green speak or give a seminar to your company, association, school, or organization, contact the address below for more information.

_____ copies of the (8.5 x 11 inches) print version of book.

_____ copies of the PDF version (per computer to use it).

Please charge my ____ Visa ____ Master Card ____ American Express
or ____ Check or Money Order.

Make checks payable and return to: Crème de la Crème Press, 2342 Shattuck Ave., No. 101, Berkeley, CA. 94704-1517, USA.
[http://www.freewebs.com/honors   Tel/Fax: 206-600-6082]

Total Amount = $_____

Name _____

Organization _____

Address _____

City/State/Zip _____

Phone _____ Email _____

Card# _____ Exp. Date _____

Signature _____